CONTENTS

THE NERVOUS PEACE

DAVID McKITTRICK

THE
BLACKSTAFF
PRESS

BELFAST

David McKittrick, who was born in Belfast, has been Ireland correspondent for the London *Independent* since 1986. He has reported on Northern Ireland and Anglo-Irish relations since 1973, principally as northern editor and London editor of the *Irish Times*. He broadcasts regularly and has contributed to a wide range of publications in Ireland, Britain and further afield. He has won a number of awards, including, jointly with Mary Holland, the Christopher Ewart-Biggs Memorial Prize. Two previous collections of his work have been published by Blackstaff Press: *Despatches from Belfast* in 1989, and *Endgame* in 1994.

First published in 1996 by
The Blackstaff Press Limited
3 Galway Park, Dundonald, Belfast BT16 0AN, Northern Ireland
© This collection, David McKittrick, 1996
All rights reserved

Typeset by Paragon Typesetters, Newton-le-Willows, Merseyside

Printed in Ireland by ColourBooks Limited

A CIP catalogue record for this book
is available from the British Library

ISBN 0-85640-575-2

PREFACE

The republican and loyalist ceasefires of 1994 and the year and a half which followed provided an intriguing and sometimes exhilarating period. It was the end of an era, the halting of the IRA's long war, but there was no agreement on why they stopped, on how genuine they were, on how the authorities should react, and on whether the peace would endure.

It was a time of great hope but also one of some trepidation, for no one could be completely confident that the ceasefires would last for ever. The articles in this collection, which first appeared in the *Independent* and the *Independent on Sunday*, not only record the ceasefires themselves and the eventful time that followed, but also illustrate something of the atmosphere of the period.

My last collection with Blackstaff Press was entitled *Endgame*, not after Samuel Beckett but because of a sense that, as in a chess game, the Troubles were entering their final phase. There is still that sense. If the ceasefires do hold, the course of events traced here will show how uncertain a period it was; if not, these articles will stand as testimony to how a historic opportunity was lost.

The articles have been tidied, edited and in some cases shortened to prevent repetition. With only a few minor exceptions they appear in strict chronological order, to convey the feeling of how the peace process developed on a week-by-week basis.

Thanks is due to many sources who cannot be named, in particular one person whom I refer to as "the Greek", whose guidance and insight have been invaluable over so many years. Thanks too to all at the *Independent*, in particular David Felton and the home desk team, and to the Blackstaff Press team for making this, our third venture together, such a pleasant and stress-free enterprise.

I would also like to thank journalists who have been of great help in various ways, including Deric Henderson, Tom Kelly, Ed Moloney, Eamonn Mallie, Fionnuala O Connor and Brian Rowan. Fionnuala and Tom read drafts of the book and offered many useful suggestions and opinions. Eamonn and Fionnuala in particular were always on hand to provide advice, argument and analysis in the most friendly way.

DAVID MCKITTRICK
BELFAST
JANUARY 1996

for Pat,
Kerry and Julie

The historic moment came just before 11 a.m. on a Wednesday morning with an IRA statement announcing that "as of midnight, August 31, there will be a complete cessation of military operations. All our units have been instructed accordingly."

Twenty-five years of death and destruction had left Northern Ireland such a tight, closed, wary society that when the announcement came it brought no spontaneous eruptions of joy.

---

1 SEPTEMBER 1994   THE INDEPENDENT

IRA declares peace

People did not dance in the streets yesterday. They said, "I'll believe it when I see it." They said, "I wonder what the murdering bastards will get out of it." They said, "It's a con." Most of these things they said to themselves, or in safe company.

To react in a particular way was a political act, which could be dangerous or look foolish. Over the years the optimists in Belfast have dwindled to a tiny band, much patronised by everyone else. For most, the carapace of cynicism is so thick that they have not yet admitted, even to themselves, the significance of the IRA's announcement.

Because of all the layers of suspicion, and because this is a zero-sum conflict, the immediate reactions were first to establish that it really is over, and second to work out who won. Unionists and the British government want it carved in tablets of stone that the stoppage really is permanent. The government in Dublin, which is a society dedicated to the culture of celebration, is satisfied already. The southern Irish are world champions at parties and revelry;

1

Sinn Féin president Gerry Adams addressing a west Belfast rally on the day the IRA announced its "complete cessation of military operations"

northern culture has always been grimmer, and a quarter of a century of division and death has done nothing to improve that.

The IRA will presumably in time satisfy London that it means what it says, but Unionists will not be convinced. They will say that since the IRA guns and Semtex are still out there somewhere, the republicans must still be regarded as an armed movement and excluded from politics. The mistrust between Unionists and republicans will last for generations.

The business was primarily between the IRA and the British government, and it is here that the business of permanency is to be sorted out. The Unionist community is poised, uncertain whether to accept the calming words of James Molyneaux, leader of the Ulster Unionists, or to believe the prophecies of treachery coming from Democratic Unionist party leader the Rev Ian Paisley.

Its final verdict on this point will help decide whether the loyalist paramilitaries open up again on Catholic pubs, or whether they decide to give the peace a chance and try to get their own boys home from the prisons. Many lives could depend on this decision. In the meantime, the point about permanency will either be quickly settled or develop into the kind of stubborn stalemate which has characterised so much of the peace process. Many lives could depend on that too.

Yet up in west Belfast, among the hundreds who turned out at a hastily arranged rally to hear Sinn Féin president Gerry Adams and Martin McGuinness, no one was in any doubt: it was over. The IRA campaign, the major part of the violence through the years, has run its course.

Gerry Adams was clapped and cheered and given flowers when he appeared. He was cheered when he said the prisoners should be released, and again when he said they would one day get their republic. He praised the IRA to the skies and praised the people of west Belfast, who remained undefeated despite all Britain had thrown at them.

But he did not claim victory; he did not tell them they had won; he said, in fact, that the core issues had not yet been resolved. This, lightly encoded, means the IRA campaign has been stopped without achieving many of its aims, including, crucially, that of extracting a British declaration of intent to withdraw.

Mr Adams and Mr McGuinness will now be arguing for this at the conference table, rather than seeking to bring it about through force. The crowd applauded, but it was all slightly forced. The Sinn Féin woman who chaired the rally, who is noted for her generally unsmiling countenance, uncharacteristically wore a fixed smile for much of the time. She told them: "One thing we all know is that the struggle is not over. We are into a new and important phase of this struggle." They dutifully applauded; they felt they had to applaud; but it was clearly putting a brave face on things.

Mr Paisley may think the republicans have won, but the people who stood in the street plainly did not. These are proud people. One of them years ago coined the phrase: "God made the Catholics and the Armalite made them equal." The new proposition being put to them by Mr Adams is that his presence in politics will fulfil the function of that Armalite. They showed much trust in him, but there is less than full commitment to his argument.

Even if the import of the day had been more clear cut, it would not have been a time for the sort of jubilation which attended, for example, the fall of the Berlin wall. There has been too much loss, too many funerals, too many widows and orphans for that type of celebration. Besides, too many issues remain unresolved, too many divisions remain, too many things could yet go wrong.

This may not be the end: there will probably be more deaths before it is all over and before armed conflict can finally be replaced by mere political controversy. But a momentous point has been passed in this painful process: the IRA has stopped and does not intend to start again.

Realists will dwell on all the things that can still go wrong, but perhaps yesterday was the day when it became safe to join the optimists and to accept – intellectually if not with joy – that Northern Ireland is moving, slowly and awkwardly but unmistakably, towards peace.

The ceasefire did not, of course, come out of the blue. It followed years of violence, argument and debate: there were many steps forward and many steps back.

Long night's journey into day

Republicans touring west Belfast on the day of the IRA cessation

On a chair beside a pink dressing table in the bedroom of a house in the backstreets of Belfast, almost exactly four years ago, sat an unmasked representative of the IRA. I sat near him on the edge of the double bed, making a verbatim note of the words he delivered in a flat near-monotone. He said this:

"We can state absolutely, on the record, that there will be no ceasefire, no truce, no 'cessation of violence' short of a British withdrawal. That, as blunt as that, is our position."

The IRA believed that in the mid-1970s the British had bluffed and conned it into a near-fatal ceasefire, a thing it swore would never be allowed to happen again. This man was doing no more than restating what had, ever since then, been a republican article of faith. But then he added: "Having said that, should the British government at any stage genuinely seek dialogue, then we are more than willing to engage in dialogue with them."

The four years since then have been packed with political developments and violent death, with exhilaration and tragedy, with hope and near-despair. Republican spokespersons have issued scores of statements, some harking back to the old hard line, some suggesting that a new beginning could be made.

Few were certain whether the hints of change were more apparent than real. It was difficult to know whether Adams was sincere, difficult to know where he was going, difficult to know whether his hidebound movement would follow where he led.

When he and Martin McGuinness deposed the old guard to take charge of the republican movement, they did so on a no-ceasefire ticket. They accused the old leaders of seeking unrealistic short cuts, declared that talk of early British withdrawal was a mirage, and impressed on their supporters that a long war lay ahead.

This new development does not mean they have ditched their cherished republican ideals. They remain dedicated to the goal of a 32-county republic, but they have been pragmatists ready to react to changed circumstances. The proposition for which they have now signed up is that progress can better be made towards their goal through political and diplomatic activity, rather than blowing up pubs and slipping boobytraps under policemen's cars.

Mr Adams has always been an innovator. First he developed Sinn Féin, which had always been a poor second cousin to the IRA, into an effective political machine. He then set it to explore a number of different directions, one of which was the process which has led to the present momentous development.

The republican movement has for many years functioned with an Armalite in one hand and a ballot paper in the other, and during that time it has discovered that the two approaches throw up many contradictions. It may well be, for example, that the republicans might have turned earlier to thoughts of ceasefires had not Libya, in the mid-1980s, showered large amounts of arms and explosives on the IRA. In the mid-1980s the terrorist organisation had been at a low ebb, but suddenly they had enough munitions to last into the 21st century.

A violent upsurge followed. The late 1980s saw a large number of soldiers killed in Northern Ireland, together with sustained offensives in Britain and on the continent. Eight soldiers died when a bomb blew up their coach at Ballygawley, Co Tyrone; six more perished when a device exploded under their van in Lisburn, Co Antrim, after they had taken part in a "fun-run". Assassinations were stepped up against alleged loyalist activists and on people such as builders who worked for the security forces.

The IRA seemed at its most dangerous ever but the security forces, as one senior republican put it, "raised their game". The SAS killed three IRA members in Gibraltar, half a dozen others in a series of ambushes, and left eight IRA men dead on the road at Loughgall in Co Armagh. But although these were considerable setbacks, the movement suffered more, in political terms, from self-inflicted wounds such as the Enniskillen Poppy Day bombing, when 11 Protestants were killed.

A local businessman, Gordon Wilson, spoke on radio of how he lay in the rubble beside his daughter Marie, a nurse, as she breathed her last. People wept as they heard him absolving her killers in an almost superhuman display of Christian forgiveness. Republican hardcore support in the northern ghettos was unfazed by such incidents but elsewhere they had crucial repercussions for Sinn Féin, especially in the Republic.

For some years the organisation had targeted the south of Ireland as its next major area of expansion, but after Enniskillen it became plain that Sinn Féin could not win Dáil seats. The people of the Republic were collectively appalled by the bombing, and Sinn Féin support there plummeted to less than 2 per cent of the vote. The road to the south became a closed avenue because of Enniskillen, just as republican links to the British left had been sundered some years earlier by the Harrods and Brighton bombings. In other words, the expanding IRA campaign collided with Sinn Féin aspirations to infiltrate southern politics, and in the end it destroyed them.

The same type of thing may have happened, on a grander scale, as the military campaign came to sit less and less easily with the developing peace process. With the collapse of the idea of winning popular support in the south, Sinn Féin leaders spoke instead of building a "pan-nationalist front" with other groupings. Their problem was, however, that the continuing IRA violence meant no other nationalist grouping of any consequence wanted anything to do with them.

In the meantime, the evolution of Sinn Féin as a political party gradually changed the character of the republican movement. Even as the violence continued, the existence of the party meant that a growing culture of debate was grafted on to the IRA's inherent militarism. Theoretical journals flourished, featuring long articles on aspects of republican ideology. Sinn Féin has many able people in its ranks: these were not peaceniks by any means, but the debates and discussions began to produce a discernible shift away from the simplistic "Brits out" line. Party policy became more complex as, for example, attempts

6

were made to find a place in republican theory for northern Protestants who had traditionally been dismissed as "pseudo-Brits" with no real national rights.

And then a new rhetoric began to emerge: the language of peace. Sinn Féin documents were given titles such as *Scenario for Peace* and *Towards a Lasting Peace*, and Mr Adams repeatedly declared his desire for an end to war. Against the background of unremitting violence, few took this very seriously. But one person who did was the leader of the Social Democratic and Labour party, John Hume. In 1988 he caused general astonishment when he held a series of formal talks with Mr Adams, the two parties exchanging lengthy documents.

This violation of the general protocol that constitutional representatives should not speak to those who supported violence brought a torrent of condemnation, but in spite of this the talks went on for some months. They eventually ended in what looked like stalemate, but an important marker had been put down: with hindsight, this episode may have sown the seeds of much of what was to follow.

The early 1990s were years of political sterility, as protracted inter-party talks opened, staggered along then fizzled out with no sign of agreement between Unionists and nationalists. Republicans and the British government harangued each other in public statements but there seemed no real movement. The violence of the IRA continued. They sent mortar bombs close to 10 Downing Street in 1991, caused massive damage with two bombs in the city of London, and devastated a series of Northern Ireland towns. The long war seemed endless.

But 1993 brought a tumult of activity and excitement and several electrifying moments. Fresh controversy broke out in April that year when it leaked out that Gerry Adams and John Hume had resumed their contacts. The storm of protest increased when they issued a delphic joint statement which critics said contained Sinn Féin language on self-determination; but a veritable tempest broke out in September when they announced they had reached agreement.

Mr Hume was denounced by a host of critics – especially in Dublin, where one newspaper portrayed him in a cartoon with blood on his hands. The air of condemnation was now tinged with real mystery, as the two leaders declined to publish the document they had agreed upon. It remains unpublished to this day, but Mr Hume argued that it held the potential for peace. Given that he and Mr Adams had been sworn enemies for years, it was almost impossible to imagine a basis on which they had suddenly reached agreement; but given Mr Hume's stature, the development was impossible to ignore.

When Mr Hume announced that he was presenting the idea to them, Dublin sources made it clear they were furious about having to handle anything bearing Mr Adams's "thumbprints". Dublin's cool reaction to the Hume–Adams initiative was followed by outright rejection from John Major, who declared in the Commons that the very thought of talking to Mr Adams "turned his stomach".

October 1993 brought the Shankill bombing. The IRA sent Thomas "Bootsie" Begley, a 24-year-old semi-literate north Belfast man, into a shop with a bomb, trying to kill loyalists in offices upstairs. The device went off prematurely and the building collapsed, leaving frantic rescue workers to scrabble at the rubble with their bare hands. In the wreckage they found the bodies of Begley and nine Protestant men, women and children.

It seemed the bombing had not only snuffed out the lives of 10 people but also written off the Irish peace process. The horror of that black weekend was so bad that Northern Ireland was plunged into despair: there seemed no realistic hope for a more peaceful future.

It was clear from the moment of the explosion that this was a bad bombing, as the whole building collapsed. But each hourly news bulletin seemed to bring worse news as the rescue operation proceeded: three dead; six dead; eight dead; ten dead; and so many of the bodies brought out were those of women and children. The IRA said its target was loyalist offices above the fish shop but the bomb, placed in a popular shop at a busy Saturday lunch time, was bound to cause civilian casualties.

For years Gerry Adams and Sinn Féin had been professing a republican desire for peace, and a talks process was under way. But how could that be reconciled with an atrocity like this? When Mr Adams carried the coffin of Begley the bomber, the republican position was condemned as hollow and hypocritical.

All over Northern Ireland social functions were cancelled as people stayed indoors and took extra security precautions. One observer said at the time: "I really don't come across anyone now who doesn't talk about how dreadful it is. You can see the fear everywhere. At mass on Sunday the priest said that police advice was for us to leave quickly, not to congregate chatting, just to get into our cars and get going."

Loyalist assassins exacted a grim revenge, machine-gunning six Catholics and one Protestant to death in a bar at Greysteel, Co Londonderry, and killing seven more in other incidents. It was one of the lowest points of the Troubles, with multiple funerals daily and an atmosphere full of fear, poison and hatred.

The initiative seemed to be dead, but then came one of those rare moments when the course of events – and possibly the course of history – suddenly changed. A great wave of popular nationalist support not only revived it but propelled it to centre stage of the Anglo-Irish scene. The most vivid, and poignant, example of this general endorsement was seen at a funeral in a Londonderry graveyard, when television cameras pictured Mr Hume weeping at the funeral of a man shot dead by loyalists. The man's daughter approached him and said: "Mr Hume, we've just buried my father. My family wants you to know that when we said the rosary around my daddy's coffin we prayed for you, for what you're trying to do to bring peace." Mr Hume nodded, clasped her hands, turned away and broke down in tears.

The strain on him was obviously intense: he was chain-smoking, pale and nervous, and clearly was not sleeping properly. He had put his entire career and reputation at risk, staking all on his judgement that he could do the seemingly impossible and persuade the IRA to give up violence. Early in November he collapsed and was rushed to hospital, where the doctors diagnosed exhaustion. In the following weeks he received 1,169 letters, notes and get-well cards, the vast majority urging him to persevere with his efforts.

Somehow the peace process survived that bleakest of moments, and that spasm of awful violence even became, in some mysterious way, a catalyst for progress. The momentum of peace picked up again and became even more determined; it was as if a community had peered over the brink of chaos, and collectively recoiled from it.

The Irish government was overwhelmed by this swell of sentiment and, literally overnight, adjusted its position. The Taoiseach, Albert Reynolds, declared that pursuing this path was now his priority: Mr Major, rather more slowly, also eventually came on board. Political activity intensified into a period of close negotiations between the two governments. Dublin argued that a substantial joint statement on Northern Ireland's future, which also addressed itself to republican concerns such as self-determination, held the potential for bringing about an IRA cessation of violence.

Then came an extraordinary development. For months there had been rumours that the government was in surreptitious contact with the republicans, but these were flatly denied by the Northern Ireland Secretary, Sir Patrick Mayhew. He had scoffed at one report: "It belongs more properly in the fantasy of spy thrillers than in real life."

But when a newspaper produced documentary evidence of such contacts, the tune changed. Sir Patrick held a press conference where, pale, tense and unhappy, he stumbled through his explanations of why he had been in protracted contact with Sinn Féin and the IRA. It turned out there had been many months of talks, messages and exchanges of papers: Martin McGuinness had even been given confidential documents on how the inter-party talks were going. The government was clearly apprehensive about how the Commons would react to all this, but in the event MPs took a relaxed view of it all and Sir Patrick, with a sigh of relief, survived.

The revelations may well have made it easier for the government to contemplate addressing Sinn Féin directly in public. Drafts of the statement winged their way back and forward across the Irish Sea as the two governments sought agreement. The outcome was December's Downing Street declaration which echoed the Hume–Adams agreement and in which the two governments laid out general principles and offered Sinn Féin entry to politics if the IRA abandoned violence.

Interest in Sinn Féin's reaction was intense. The republicans clearly regarded the declaration as something of a curate's egg, but instead of rejecting it they asked for clarification of its terms. The Dublin government obligingly provided extensive amplification, but Mr Major declared that no clarification was necessary and demanded an immediate response.

Weeks passed in stalemate, with momentum draining away from the process. But February brought a blaze of publicity for Gerry Adams when, in the teeth of opposition from both the British government and the American State Department, he was granted a visa to allow him to spend a few days in New York. This was a striking demonstration of the power of Irish-America.

Then came setbacks for the peace process. The IRA staged a series of "spectacular" attacks on Heathrow airport, aimed at demonstrating its violent capacity and to stress that it was not engaging in the process because of military weakness. In April, under pressure from all sides to react, it declared a ceasefire: but it was only three days long and was almost universally denounced as pitifully inadequate. Yet even as the rest of the world derided the move, within the IRA itself it represented a crossing of the Rubicon. It meant that the old position, as set out by the man beside the pink dressing table, had been overturned.

It was not until May that the British government finally issued detailed clarification of the declaration, but by this stage many assumed the life had gone from the process. This impression was further strengthened by a conference at Letterkenny, Co Donegal, in July, when Sinn Féin finally gave its response to the declaration. This was widely regarded as negative.

At that point many assumed it was all over, but then speculation steadily mounted that a substantial ceasefire was on the cards. There were repeated reports, which republicans did nothing to discourage, that a stoppage of around three months was likely. It now seems that the negativity of Letterkenny was not what the republicans wanted to convey: rather, they had wished to project that they thought it enough to work on.

This has probably been the case ever since the declaration was issued. A movement which was still committed to the old ways would have rejected the document out of hand; the fact that the republicans did not immediately say no made it inevitable, some would argue, that they would eventually say yes.

Republicans are adamant that they have not been in contact, direct or indirect, with the British government in recent months. But there does seem to have been heavy traffic, through intermediaries, with Dublin and it would not come as a surprise to discover in the future that the IRA and London had ways of establishing each other's concerns. One of the lessons of this saga is that there are generally things going on of which the public and the media know nothing.

At some point during the summer the IRA seems to have sat down and arrived at the conclusion that the time had come to go for it or forget it; and that a three-month stoppage might bring short-term tactical benefits but would only postpone the day of final decision. Such a move might well have put the British government under pressure to respond, but London and Dublin were emphatic in laying down that nothing short of a permanent end to the campaign would be enough to secure full republican entry into politics.

It may never be known whether, at the start of the peace process, Gerry Adams and his associates envisaged that it would lead to the ending of the IRA campaign on terms very different from those specified by the man beside the pink dressing table. But what is clear is that this is not an IRA surrender. The organisation has the guns, the expertise and the recruits to go on killing: it has not been militarily defeated. Rather, it has allowed itself to be persuaded that it now stands a better chance of furthering its aims through politics.

These may be violent people, but they are also proud people, with high self-esteem, who over decades have had much violence inflicted on them. What has led them to this point is not the activities of the army, the SAS, the RUC or the intelligence agencies: it is a sense that a real alternative to terrorism is on offer. This was summed up by Gerry Adams when he said: "I am satisfied that Irish nationalism, if properly mobilised and focused, at home and internationally, now has sufficient political confidence, weight and support to bring about the changes which are essential to a just and lasting peace."

In essence, the events of the last two years or so have served to convince the republicans that a cessation would not lead to their being treated as defeated and vanquished. First John Hume spoke to them; then the Irish government conquered its initial distaste for Mr Adams's thumbprints; then prominent Irish-Americans gave them a glimpse of important new areas of potential support across the Atlantic.

Sinn Féin began to think in terms of real politics, and in doing so reached an unmistakable psychological point where it began to focus on the big picture. The stark choice republicans faced this summer was that of a return to the old way where they yielded considerable negative power through their bombs and bullets, but in doing so excluded themselves from the councils of power.

The Dublin government, Irish-Americans and above all Mr Hume took grave risks in helping to bring them to this point. Many more risks and difficulties lie ahead, but at this moment there are grounds to hope that we are finally witnessing the beginning of the end of the Troubles.

The fact that the IRA declared a complete cessation, rather than the three-month suspension of violence which had been expected, took many, not least the British government, by surprise. Suddenly, whole new vistas of opportunities – and problems – opened up.

1 SEPTEMBER 1994   THE INDEPENDENT

Delicate balance of risks and opportunities

While there have been IRA ceasefires in the past, most of them in the distant past, the situation facing Northern Ireland at the moment is without exact precedent. Partly because of this, it is a moment alive with both opportunities and dangers.

The ending of the IRA campaign will pose a great many logistical and political problems. While the ceasefire is itself a momentous step, it will take a great deal of luck, judgement, good will and co-operative effort to get through the coming days and weeks safely.

The most immediate question may be that of how the government handles opinion in the loyalist community which, according to Unionist politicians and Protestant clergymen, is currently in a state of high anxiety. The traditional lurking fear of a sell-out by Britain has risen to the surface, and the view is widespread among loyalists that the IRA would not have come to this point had it not received secret concessions from Britain.

Government ministers can be expected to offer repeated assurances that this is not the case, but loyalist politicians say their credibility on this point has been severely dented by revelations that the government had extensive contacts with the republicans.

Protestant reaction could take a number of forms. The violent Ulster Defence Association has just announced that it is out for blood, a threat which everyone

12

takes seriously. Since its victims are usually drawn at random from the Catholic community the security forces have found it impossible to protect every possible target.

This situation could change, however, if the army and police were abruptly freed from what they have always seen as their main task, that of coping with the IRA campaign. In the absence of republican violence a large number of troops and policemen would suddenly be available for anti-loyalist activity.

At the same time, the security forces will have to take care in how they go about such work. If Protestant anxieties remain high, the residents of hardline loyalist districts may not take kindly to the sight of a heavy police presence in their areas, especially if the republican ghettos are said to be only lightly policed.

On the political front, Unionist representatives will be maintaining the most intense scrutiny of any move which has the appearance of being a concession to the republicans – or indeed to the Irish government, for advances made by constitutional nationalists are also worrying to Unionist opinion.

The Rev Ian Paisley, although prepared to see Mr Major, has for some months refused to meet the Northern Ireland Secretary, Sir Patrick Mayhew. Unionists have often used boycotts in the past, and if the situation heats up considerably over the next week it would come as no surprise to see an extension of the tactic.

One of the Unionist nightmares is for the emergence of a formidable, non-violent pan-nationalist front which would include the Irish government, the SDLP, important Irish-Americans and a newly pacific Sinn Féin. Unionists have little confidence that the British government would stand up to the political and diplomatic strength of such an alliance, all singing, for a change, from much the same hymn sheet.

The Unionist psyche is full of dark fears and lurking suspicions. The legacies of history and geography mean that they are subject to an uncertainty that at the best of times borders on the chronic. This means that the average Unionist politician is, naturally enough, opposed to the IRA campaign when the republicans are killing people and doing damage; but is also, paradoxically, suspicious of ceasefires because he sees other dangers there.

The Unionist community has lived through 25 deeply unhappy years as the IRA campaign continued and as, in its eyes, nationalists made gain after gain. Its leaders believe that most of those advances have come about because of IRA violence, but that other gains have resulted from political activity by John Hume and the Irish government.

Seen from this perspective, it hardly matters whether the nationalists make progress through terrorism or diplomacy, because in either case the Unionist cause suffers. Loyalist paramilitary leaders privately speak of John Hume with more or less the same hatred as they reserve for Gerry Adams.

On reason is because many Unionists believe Hume and Adams have formulated coherent philosophies while Unionism is characterised by uncertainty about which direction it should take. Earlier this year a senior Ulster Unionist MP, addressing a public meeting in the Shankill Road district of Belfast, spent several minutes explaining that what Unionism desperately needed was a Big Idea.

His analysis was that Unionists always had their backs to the wall; that they needed something to get them off the defensive; that they required a new approach that would be pro-active rather than perpetually reactive. Then he paused and said: "Unfortunately, I've no idea what this might be."

Unionism's misfortune is that no one else in its ranks knows what it should be either. Within months politicians are expected to enter the deepest and most far-reaching negotiation in Northern Ireland's history, and all the signs are that Unionism will be found lacking, both in terms of its personnel and the lack of that Big Idea.

Its traditional insistence that Northern Ireland is British and nothing else has been left behind by events. With the Anglo-Irish agreement in 1985 Britain redefined the problem, to the dismay of Unionists, in an Anglo-Irish context.

London has held to that view ever since, right through the special relationship which Ulster Unionist leader James Molyneaux is said to have developed with Mr Major. On the one hand the Prime Minister has made some encouraging noises about the union, but on the other he has maintained his close relationship with Dublin; he sanctioned two years of secret talks with the IRA; and he persevered with the idea of offering Sinn Féin entry into politics.

Mr Molyneaux favoured none of these approaches. The Prime Minister was aware of this, and acutely aware too of the nine potentially useful Commons votes he commands; yet those policies were maintained. Mr Molyneaux quietly and doggedly pursued his own esoteric agenda, based on his incomprehensible belief that altering obscure parliamentary procedures will strengthen the union and is the best way to advance the Unionist cause.

While the Ulster Unionist leader concentrated on such minutiae as whether legislation should be by Bill or Order in Council, momentous events such as the Downing Street declaration and the IRA cessation have been changing the course of Irish politics. This could be a metaphor for the state of Unionism itself, which is in danger of being left behind by the tide of history.

With Sinn Féin, John Hume's SDLP, the Irish government and Irish-America all involved in the coming negotiations, they will clearly go to the fundamentals of the Irish question; and all four of those elements will be represented by formidable negotiators.

Mr Molyneaux has little taste for negotiation or for innovation, which is hardly surprising in a man who last week celebrated his 74th birthday. Other senior figures in his party, such as his possible successors John Taylor, David

Trimble and William Ross, have little experience in negotiating and show no sign of having a Big Idea.

Unionism, in fact, is deeply split at the moment. For almost a decade Mr Molyneaux maintained a close relationship with the Rev Ian Paisley, but this broke up amid considerable bitterness earlier this year. Mr Paisley, who once admired Mr Molyneaux, has since compared him to Neville Chamberlain and even Judas Iscariot.

Mr Paisley himself, at 68, shows no signs of shedding the negative approach of a lifetime and trying to reach an accommodation. Behind him stand the Rev William McCrea, who is if anything even more in the "not an inch" mould than his leader, and Peter Robinson, who has occasionally gone through moderate phases but is now judged to have shot his bolt.

The balance of forces on the nationalist side is intriguing. Mr Adams has, in a dramatic gamble, brought about an IRA cessation of violence without achieving his movement's historic aims. It remains to be seen whether Sinn Féin's traditional voters stay with the party in its new pacific role or become demoralised and drift away. The probability is that Mr Adams's exceptionally high standing within the republican community will hold it together.

The standing of John Hume among constitutional nationalists is even higher. In the European elections in the springtime he recorded his biggest ever vote, almost surpassing that of Mr Paisley. That was when he was trying to bring about an IRA cessation; now that it has actually happened he has assumed a place in the nationalist pantheon comparable to that of O'Connell and Parnell at their zenith.

All of this means that nationalist representatives will be going into negotiations with high hopes and high expectations while Unionists will be nervous and fearful. Unionism has failed in its efforts to get the genie back into the bottle and have the issue treated as an internal UK issue. Nationalists have succeeded in establishing both Anglo-Irish and American dimensions. The absence of a Unionist Big Idea will now be painfully obvious, and could cost that community dear.

The IRA ceasefire was followed by much uncertainty, with the unanswered questions of whether it was permanent and how the loyalist paramilitary groups would react. In the meantime, the atmosphere relaxed a little.

Basking in sunshine and hope

The two policemen basked in the autumn sunshine of Belfast, relaxed and chatting to each other. Their standard RUC revolvers were strapped to their sides but they carried no rifles and had removed their tunics to enjoy the sun.

They had also taken off their flak jackets, and there they stood on the Falls Road, just opposite Divis Flats where so many soldiers and policemen have been killed and injured over the last 25 years.

Not far away stood three of their colleagues, clearly belt-and-braces men: they wore no tunics but, just in case, they sported flak jackets over their shirts. It was day one of the IRA ceasefire, and already things were changing in west Belfast.

Further up the road something else had changed. On a large and prominent gable wall, which nobody travelling along the Falls could fail to notice, three men were working on the latest republican mural. One painted while another held the ladder and a third sat on an abandoned mattress having a smoke and calling out helpful suggestions.

This new work shows a series of building bricks bearing words such as unity, freedom, justice for all and amnesty for political prisoners. The topmost brick is marked peace.

There have been scores of wall paintings in west Belfast but this one had a profound significance which will not be lost on local people. This is because it covers a previous work which glorified the three members of the IRA shot dead by the SAS in Gibraltar: in one coat of paint the message has been transformed from the cult of martyrdom to a new and constructive image. A new tone is being set.

In the loyalist backstreets, however, the grimmer message was one of business as usual. "Kill all pan nationalists," one new scrawl proclaimed. Another warned: "The battle is only starting – UVF."

Over in republican Ardoyne an army foot patrol moved through the mean streets, keeping to a familiar routine. A squaddie crouched himself into a ball at a street corner, as squaddies have been trained to do for 25 years, to present as small a target as possible.

But after a few minutes he stood up and moved a couple of feet away from the wall, standing in full view in the street. His gaze remained wary, however: the atmosphere is already lightening, but nobody in Belfast is completely relaxing, just yet.

As the security forces attempted to adapt to the new situation, so too did the republican grassroots.

4 SEPTEMBER 1994   THE INDEPENDENT

Waving goodbye to simple answers

"Wave bye-bye to the Brits," the republican woman said to the child in her arms, at the end of the rally on the Falls Road, and the blond youngster obligingly waved towards the RUC–army base. It was impossible to work out whether she really thought the police and troops would all be leaving, or was indulging in a moment of fantasy before returning to the unpalatable reality that the IRA had stopped without securing a British withdrawal.

This rally was an important occasion for Sinn Féin, for the republicans have been carefully gauging reaction to the IRA's ceasefire decision, and it is taking some time for some of its more profound implications to sink in.

Gerry Adams had to strike a precisely measured tone in his speech. He is the man who has gradually taken the word "victory" out of the republican vocabulary and replaced it with the word "peace". He got his usual warm reception, for these people, the republican grassroots, really do adore him. The crowd, of fewer than a thousand, was just about respectable for such an event, but was not an exceptionally big turnout by republican standards.

The Adams vocabulary has long been accepted by his followers, but although the word peace has been adopted the concept has not been fully absorbed by all of them. Not all of them have learnt to think in terms of a settlement rather

17

than victory; a fair few, for example, presume Mr Adams has struck a secret deal with the British which will before long give them victory.

In his short speech he felt the need to stress that the IRA was not split on the ceasefire decision. In a passage which was unusually explicit for a Sinn Féin spokesman he declared: "A united Irish Republican Army, a united army of the people, is saying to the British government, let's have peace." He was concerned to reassure his people rather than to claim victory. Sinn Féin would be insisting in any negotiations on "the need to build a united and independent Ireland," he said: "All of our objectives are winnable – remember that, every one of our objectives is winnable." He very definitely did not tell them they had won.

He then marched his people, in relaxed mood, round to the Springfield Road RUC–army base where they sang "We shall overcome" while a man painted "Time to go" on the reinforced steel wall. Down the country, meanwhile, other republicans were symbolically reopening a road which had been closed by the army.

The crowd outside the base waved goodbye at the base, and a soldier at an upstairs window waved back, apparently good-naturedly. He may have been reflecting that he would rather be confronted by some street-theatre and a drop of paint than a rocket attack.

A man in the crowd asked me: "Well, do we look like we're defeated?" They did not; but nor did they look as though they had won. The IRA campaign was ended voluntarily, leaving the republicans neither victorious nor beaten. They looked like people coming to grips with the fact that the campaign has ended on a note which few expected, which has challenged many of their own assumptions, and which has created new uncertainties which will last for years to come.

The ceasefire was quickly followed by the first in a series of historic handshakes. Although the British government continued to question whether the IRA's campaign was really over, Dublin moved swiftly to demonstrate that it accepted the IRA and Sinn Féin at their word.

The Taoiseach, Albert Reynolds, together with John Hume, met Gerry Adams in Dublin, the first time since the Irish civil war period in the 1920s that such an encounter had taken place. The three men issued a statement in which they said: "We are at the beginning of a new era in which we are all totally and absolutely committed to democratic and peaceful methods of resolving our political problems."

Then they stepped out of Mr Reynolds's office to meet a large assemblage of cameras, television crews and press people.

---

7 SEPTEMBER 1994   THE INDEPENDENT

Sinn Féin returns to the fold

They handled it pretty well, this little moment in history, this instant with its possibility of new beginnings and new directions in Irish history. They were suitably grave as they came down the ornate steps of the Taoiseach's office, with its elaborate entrance and its grand columns.

Albert Reynolds, the Taoiseach, shook the hand of Gerry Adams, leader of Sinn Féin, then both shook the hand of John Hume, leader of the SDLP, who had helped bring them together.

Mr Reynolds, in his familiar persona of a brisk no-nonsense businessman,

Nationalism's Big Three – Gerry Adams, Albert Reynolds and John Hume – shake hands to cement the peace

might have been closing a deal with a commercial partner. Mr Adams, whose party has not been officially welcomed by a Dublin government for 25 years, exuded the personal dignity which so infuriates his opponents. Not so long ago Mr Reynolds regarded Mr Adams as a subversive, while Mr Adams thought of the Irish government as quislings and the puppets of Britain.

It was a moment of history, but there are so many precedents of welcoming violent prodigals into politics that the Irish reckon they know instinctively how to deal with such events. The drill is not to stand on ceremony or dwell on formalities, not to indulge in recriminations, but to get the miscreants in before they change their minds.

Mr Reynolds's own Fianna Fáil party went through just such a transformation in the 1920s and 1930s. At least two of his predecessors as Fianna Fáil leader and Taoiseach had a good working knowledge of Mauser and Lee-Enfield rifles before rising to the highest office in Irish politics. One of them famously described Fianna Fáil as "a slightly constitutional party".

Only six days after the IRA laid down its arms, Mr Adams has been accepted into the political fold by nationalist Ireland, an event marked by this unprecedented handshake. But this being Ireland, and this being such a protracted and painful peace process, the meeting was also a symbol of discord.

David Trimble of the Ulster Unionist party said it was held in "indecent, obscene haste", while it is obvious that the British government still officially regards Sinn Féin as, at best, an only slightly constitutional party. So this historic moment still left open the question of when London will come to agree with Dublin that the IRA's 25-year war is over.

After the initial excitement, controversy and confusion generated by the IRA ceasefire, the realisation dawned that ahead lay a long, hard road strewn with many obstacles.

19 SEPTEMBER 1994   THE INDEPENDENT

The long road to peace

Last week RUC officers set up a crime prevention advice stand in the Park Centre, a large shopping complex just inside nationalist west Belfast. Local Sinn Féin members reacted angrily, staging a placard protest and describing the RUC as an unacceptable police force.

It was a tiny incident, but also a telling sign of how quickly and profoundly change is coming to Northern Ireland. Three weeks ago any such RUC operation would have been highly unlikely, since it invited a potentially lethal IRA action. Today republicans still do not like it, but their objections take the form of protests rather than rocket attacks.

Northern Ireland is now facing a new phase where many of the ground rules,

Despite the cessation, divisions and suspicions remained: work on this peaceline continued even after the IRA ceasefire

some trivial and some fundamental, are going to change. Few realise just how profound the changes are going to be, and just how many things might go wrong.

The IRA ceasefire, though a momentous move, was only one step along a complicated, precarious and painful road to peace. It clearly opens an important window of opportunity, but it also opens up a whole new vista of problems to be addressed.

There are many more questions than answers. Will the violent loyalists declare their own ceasefire? Will they and the IRA hand in their weaponry? How can the formidable security apparatus be gradually dismantled? Will prisoners be released early? How can a security economy be transformed into a normal one? And can sworn enemies ever get round a table and hammer out a lasting settlement?

Some problems may melt away and cause surprisingly little trouble, while others have the capacity to flare up into sticking points. And always there is the possibility of the unforeseen: the unpredicted political development, or series of events, or acts of violence, which might derail the whole process.

Pessimists can point to the number and scale of the problems and wonder how all of them can possibly be dealt with. Optimists will argue that elsewhere in the world other conflicts with even greater problems have been effectively resolved. One thing is, however, clear: success will require both increased good will and determination, both judgement and luck.

DEMILITARISATION

High on the wall of a house in Bombay Street, not far from the Falls Road, hangs a plaque dedicated to the memory of Gerald McAuley, a 15-year-old member of the IRA's junior wing. McAuley was shot dead by a loyalist intruder in August 1969, when the street was the scene of bitter fighting between Catholics and Protestants.

A Protestant mob from the Shankill invaded the district, destroying almost 50 of the little terraced houses with petrol bombs and attacking Clonard monastery, which stands at the end of the street. Both sides had a few guns, there was much shooting, and dozens of people were injured.

A priest, Father McLaughlin, later told a tribunal headed by Lord Scarman what it was like: "I was terribly agitated and worked up, and terribly afraid there was going to be a holocaust and that the whole area was going to be wiped out. I was absolutely convinced that this was an attempt not merely to wipe out the monastery but the whole area. I was really in desperation for help."

The priest testified that he came across two armed men, "both known to him as reliable", in a lower corridor of the monastery. They told him they would defend the building and, "because of the fear of an attack, the rumour about a sniper and the absence of police", he allowed them to stay. He instructed them "to use their weapons as a last resort if the monastery was being attacked, and then only to fire in the air".

Bombay Street remains the great symbol of Catholic families at the mercy of marauding loyalists, but similar scenes were enacted elsewhere in 1969. In all 1,500 Catholic families were displaced, compared with 315 Protestant families. More than 5 per cent of Catholic families in Belfast had to move house.

Young McAuley was hailed as a hero for giving his life in trying to keep the loyalists at bay. But the IRA was bitterly criticised for not carrying out its traditional role of defending Catholic areas against loyalist attack.

Bombay Street was in a real sense the birthplace of the Provisional IRA, which shortly afterwards broke away from the main IRA under the slogan "From the ashes of Bombay Street rose the Provisionals". They vowed that vulnerable Catholic areas would never again be left undefended.

It is this singular genesis which makes it extremely unlikely that, whatever pressures are put on it in the months ahead, the IRA will hand over a single gun. While republicans have regularly called for a complete demilitarisation, they will probably argue that they cannot be expected to carry out unilateral disarmament while there are so many other guns still out there.

Northern Ireland's population of a million and a half people holds no fewer than 120,000 legally held firearms, most of which are in Protestant hands. Violent loyalist groups have many other weapons, which they have used over the years to kill about 900 Catholics. These groups may declare a ceasefire, but there is no sign they are prepared to surrender their guns. The question is therefore whether the peace process can move on while all the weapons are still out there, or whether it will stall on this point.

This issue is likely to be the thorniest of what is described as the demilitarisation process, but it will not be the only difficulty. There have been several reports of beatings in republican areas since the announcement of the IRA ceasefire, and the organisation is being pressed to clarify whether it was responsible for these.

It also has yet to say whether the hundreds of people it has banished from Northern Ireland over the years are now free to return without the threat of violence. Most of these were forced out for their alleged involvement in drugs, joyriding, crime or other activities defined by the IRA as "anti-social activities".

One genuine fear in republican districts – which is also shared by at least one senior policeman – is that a large-scale reappearance of such people will lead to a crime wave. In particular Belfast has an unusually small hard-drug problem, partly because the IRA threatened to kill drug dealers: the concern is that the city might now be at the mercy of the pushers.

This raises the question of whether residents in republican districts, many of whom have a strong sense of community and self-help, will begin to think in terms of some form of vigilantism. For the RUC, coping with a potential crime wave will be an early challenge and an opportunity to show whether it can meet community concerns.

Another major issue concerns the IRA's financial structure, which according to the RUC, manages to raise millions of pounds each year despite all the efforts of the authorities. No one knows whether the intention is to keep this structure intact, let it wither away, or perhaps to burrow it into the republican community in some modified form.

In all of this the question of IRA prisoners will be crucial. There are 900 of these in jail in Northern Ireland, and the IRA's attitude is that it is inconceivable to think of violence ending with hundreds of its members left to spend long years behind bars.

Mr Major has already specifically ruled out an amnesty but the question of early releases is very much in the air, particularly since the Irish government last week indicated that some IRA members held in the south would not serve their full sentences.

Loyalist paramilitary sources have already signalled that they have no objection to early releases, since the 450 loyalists behind bars would clearly stand to benefit from any such move.

More immediately, much work will be involved in the task of dismantling the formidable security apparatus which has been built up over the last quarter-century. If the IRA ceasefire is followed by similar moves from the tiny INLA (Irish National Liberation Army) and the loyalists, Northern Ireland will suddenly have a surfeit of security force installations and personnel.

At the moment well over 100 border roads remain closed, while many roads and streets in the cities and towns are also sealed off on either a temporary or a permanent basis. Both town and country are studded with heavily fortified bases and lookout posts: in Belfast three substantial military installations are perched on top of high-rise flats.

If the peace becomes permanent most of these will no longer be needed. A large-scale building programme now under way to modernise army and police bases will have to be reviewed; and clearly there will be no further need for many of the 30,000-plus people employed in the security field.

Exactly how many security bases and how many troops and police will be needed is presently a matter of guesswork, but there will certainly be closures and redundancies. Too many job losses, inflicted too quickly, could have sharp effects on both the economy and on the political situation; but too slow a down-scaling process will do nothing to improve the acceptability of the RUC in nationalist districts.

Far-reaching debate on policing structures will figure in future political negotiations, but in the meantime day-to-day policing has to go on. The handling of the process of demilitarisation will have vital effects on the general atmosphere, and could significantly help or hinder the overall peace process.

LOYALIST PARAMILITARIES

A major part of the jigsaw still to be slotted into place is in the hands of the loyalist paramilitary groups, who have yet to give their definitive response to the IRA ceasefire.

Although loyalist violence has continued, it has done so at a much lower level since the ceasefire, and sources close to the Protestant paramilitants have hinted that a stoppage is probably on the way.

One source said: "The bottom line is that these people realise it would be ridiculous for them to keep on fighting when the IRA has stopped. It just wouldn't make any sense." The general assessment is that once the IRA and INLA have stopped, it will be a major surprise if the loyalist campaign has not been called off by Christmas at the latest.

At the same time, it may well be that the loyalist ceasefire, when it comes, will be of a different character to the IRA cessation. The republicans were anxious to secure a place at the conference table and recognised this could only happen with a complete ending of their campaign.

Loyalist groups, by contrast, do not have the same ambition to get into mainstream politics, and their leaders show no signs of wishing to disband their organisations. They may therefore declare that they are ceasing offensive activities but will remain in existence to defend the loyalist cause if that should prove necessary in the future.

This means they will, if they can, continue to be a force in the loyalist ghettos, where they have a financial machine based on pubs, clubs and other activities, many of them illegal. In the event of lasting peace some members may drift away, but many of the leaders will be intent on preserving their status as men of power in the backstreets.

POLITICAL TALKS

All the signs are that keeping the peace process alive and moving forward will entail not months but years of political talks, manoeuvring and controversies.

The government's private assessment is that all-inclusive round-table negotiations involving London, Dublin and the political parties are probably two years away. The Irish government and the Clinton administration will undoubtedly be seeking faster progress, but there is so much ground to cover that the process will inevitably be a lengthy one.

In political terms the Irish government is moving at some speed with the aim of opening its Forum for Peace and Reconciliation in Dublin next month. Sinn Féin will be included in this but the Unionist parties will turn down invitations to attend.

In the meantime the Irish and British governments are hoping to produce a "framework document" in about a month's time, setting out their view of the future. John Major has stressed that this will not be a blueprint, but it is expected to outline the general views of the two governments.

Beyond that lies the task of easing Sinn Féin fully into the political processes. Once the government has accepted the IRA cessation as permanent, there will be exploratory talks, which Sinn Féin says it expects to begin well before Christmas. Given that these contacts will touch on matters such as the handing in of arms and other highly controversial topics, progress will not be easy.

One large unknown factor underlying all of this is the state of opinion within the republican movement. At the moment it appears solidly behind Gerry Adams in the momentous move of ending IRA violence, but there are many republican precedents for the emergence of ultras who refuse to give up the use of force.

Assuming any such tendency can be dealt with, many months of work clearly lie ahead before the demilitarisation process is settled, and before Sinn Féin can enter conventional politics.

If all that is achieved, there will then come the task of shepherding all the elements involved into inclusive talks. It is difficult ever to imagine a handshake between Mr Adams and the Rev Ian Paisley, but the intention is, possibly using some arm's-length device, to have them engaged in the same talks process with the aim of reaching an agreed political settlement.

Even to picture a dialogue between the two men is to open up an entirely new vista of entirely new problems. Are they, and the British government, ever to agree on Northern Ireland's constitutional position, on Dublin's role, on an equality agenda, on new structures of policing?

At this moment, it has to be said that the obstacles to ultimate success in all of this are formidable: but it must also be pointed out that just a month ago there seemed literally no chance of success at all. Substantial progress, therefore, has already been made, and with that has come hope that the idea of eventual lasting peace is no longer an impossible dream.

Although the guns and bombs fell silent, it became clear within weeks of the IRA ceasefire that a form of unarmed savagery was set to continue in the republican ghettos.

30 SEPTEMBER 1994   THE INDEPENDENT

From guns to iron bars

A photograph in the *Belfast Telegraph* graphically showed the effects of an IRA punishment beating. Gavin Smyth, a 16-year-old from Andersonstown, was pictured propped up in a hospital bed, his bandaged legs stretched out before him.

His hands were clasped together, his eyes closed in pain. Bloodstains oozed through his bandages, indicating the spots where both his legs were broken by the punishment squad. His father, Seamus Smyth, said: "They used an iron bar. They got him to roll over three times so that they could attack his legs from every side."

I discussed the photograph with a middle-aged woman from west Belfast: neither of us knew Gavin Smyth, or what "crimes" his attackers accused him of. She declared with great feeling: "I think it's awful, really awful. Some of the injuries to these boys are horrific: some of them will be maimed for the rest of their lives."

And then she added: "It's very barbaric, but people are in a quandary. We don't want people kneecapped or shot or beaten up, but the police are doing absolutely nothing about the hoods.

"You have to live here to understand what people have to put up with. It's unbelievable: breaking into people's houses and beating up 70-year-olds, joyriders tormenting old people half the night. You'd be afraid that if the IRA did nothing the hoods would get out of hand altogether."

The woman's views are typical of a sizeable section of the community in Catholic west Belfast. Many acknowledge that these are brutal practices, but many do not trust the RUC as a police force. They generally acknowledge, too, that kneecappings and beatings have not stopped the joyriding; but they fear that ending the brutality could produce an unrestrained crime spree.

The extent to which such attitudes permeate west Belfast may be judged from the fact that the woman quoted is a nurse in the Royal Victoria Hospital. She is not involved in caring for Gavin Smyth, but she has nursed many victims of punishment shootings and beatings.

She said: "So many times nurses have gone to the car park after coming off duty, and their cars were away or the radios were gone. One time a nurse had her car broken into, the radio pulled out, stuff taken and a lot of damage done. The boy who did it stole another car and crashed it, and she ended up nursing the boy who wrecked her car. She treated him civilly but afterwards she said if she'd had a rope she'd have strung him up.

"In the ward you find some of them you can try to reason with, but the majority of them are cheeky wee bastards. Some of them say they didn't deserve what they got, others boast and brag about what they did. A lot have very sad lives, and they're more to be pitied. They won't take help; but they can't be allowed to terrorise people."

Since the IRA ceasefire on 31 August, kneecappings have ended, but the punishment beatings have actually increased. Prior to the ceasefire, the IRA this year carried out 55 kneecappings and six beatings, but Gavin Smyth is one of seven youths and men who since then have been severely beaten by squads using baseball bats, iron bars, pickaxe handles and in one case a cudgel studded with nails.

The IRA has neither confirmed nor denied responsibility for these incidents, but there is little doubt they carried out the attacks. They follow a tradition of such IRA actions, sometimes involving up to 20 men, working together with military precision. When asked, republican spokesmen tend to reply elliptically that communities have a right to defend themselves.

What the IRA announced on 31 August was "a complete cessation of military operations". Since then there has been a total absence of republican bombings and shootings: soldiers, police officers and other former IRA assassination targets have been able to relax.

But although the campaign against the crown may be over it is clear that the organisation has no intention of disbanding or becoming inactive. The IRA is still out there in the backstreets, carrying iron bars rather than Kalashnikovs; its guns may be silent but they are not to be handed over; its structure is to remain in being, for the foreseeable future at least.

The key concept here lies in the phrase "complete cessation of military operations". The IRA has not surrendered, or sought terms from the British government; it has not promised to disband, or to go legal; it has merely disengaged.

So what will the average IRA man do all day under the new order? No one yet knows. The organisation is currently in the business of defining which activities it intends to maintain. Its "policing department" – the men with the iron bars – is obviously still in operation. It is not clear whether its "procurement operations department" – the men who rob the banks – will stay in business.

The IRA runs a sizeable financial empire which, according to the security forces, has raised millions of pounds each year. Money will continue to be needed for the welfare of the hundreds of IRA prisoners and for other purposes, although large amounts will no longer need to be spent on trying to buy more weaponry abroad.

There is no talk of dissolving the financial section, and the likelihood is that it will remain in being in modified form. The organisation is involved in running pubs and clubs and has been linked to money-raising operations such as video pirating; and it would be no surprise to find it has literally millions salted away somewhere in the money markets.

The IRA's leaders may see little point in winding all this up and throwing its men out of work: the devil, after all, makes work for idle hands, and disbanding the organisation would make the emergence of violent splinter groups much more likely.

There has been much government propaganda about racketeering and Mafia-like activities, but in fact the republican community is very clear about what is and is not permissible in the way of fund-raising. The key concept is that of the victimless crime.

Sinn Féin supporters in west Belfast would not tolerate IRA involvement in, for example, local break-ins or drug dealing or any such acts which would harm the local community. But nobody much minds if the IRA runs clubs, or extracts funds from major businesses outside the area, or illegally copies videos: all these are, in west Belfast terms, victimless crimes.

There will obviously be changes in the republican financial systems, but the new rules and patterns have yet to emerge. With the IRA no longer required to finance a guerrilla war, it could redirect some of its energies into job-creation schemes for republicans. Some radical thinkers even argue that would, in the long term, be a rather healthy development, with the swords very gradually being turned into ploughshares.

Gerry Adams's comment in America, when he said a militant new IRA could emerge in a few years' time if the causes of conflict were not resolved, can be read either as a threat or as an observation based on many considerable historical precedents. It will lead some to suspect that the IRA is simply lying doggo in the expectation that its campaign of terrorism will be restarted in the coming weeks or months.

But that is not the feeling in west Belfast, where everyone, including the security forces, has psychologically come to terms with the fact that it really is all over. The ceasefire is not viewed as an experiment but as the irrevocable beginning of a completely new phase.

The cessation was in republican terms a momentous leap in the dark, based partly on the proposition that republicans could make more progress politically than militarily. But there is still an IRA, and it will continue in being.

These are early days, but the hope is that this is a transition period, and that the republicans can be pressurised into abandoning the brutality of the punishments. But Ireland has too long a history of paramilitary movements, republican and loyalist, for it to be imagined that they can disappear overnight.

One of the crucial issues to be worked out in the political negotiations ahead is that of policing, for there is presently no consensus on who should police areas such as west Belfast, and how. It will plainly be difficult to achieve agreement on this most contentious of issues, but until it comes about youths will continue to end up in hospital with shattered limbs, and nurses will continue secretly to condone the barbarism of the men with the iron bars.

The IRA ceasefire was followed by six weeks of anxious waiting to see whether the extreme Protestant groups would follow suit. During this period loyalist organisations kept up their violence but there were also signs of debate and new thinking in their camp.

The result emerged in mid-October when the loyalists announced an unconditional ceasefire. They even went further than the IRA by including a note of contrition, expressing "abject and true remorse" for all deaths of innocent victims.

The ceasefire announcement was read out by Gusty Spence.

---

14 OCTOBER 1994   THE INDEPENDENT

Loyalist icon proclaims peace

The Northern Ireland Troubles reached a point of circularity – and hopefully finality – when yesterday's loyalist ceasefire statement was delivered by one of Belfast's living icons, Augustus "Gusty" Spence.

The news that the loyalist campaign was over came from the man regarded as the first loyalist assassin jailed in the Troubles, for Gusty Spence served more than 18 years of a life sentence for the murder of a Catholic youth in 1966.

But although he was for years regarded as a symbol of violence, he made a dramatic switch in the 1970s and has for more than a decade and a half been preaching an end to conflict. He has thus become one of the most intriguing minor figures of the past quarter-century.

Spence and two other men received life imprisonment for the UVF murder

Gusty Spence, paramilitant turned peacemaker, together with other loyalist political figures

of Peter Ward, an 18-year-old Catholic barman shot dead as he left a Shankill Road pub in June 1966. Spence has always denied involvement in the killing but admits he was a UVF activist.

At the time almost everyone, including other extreme loyalists, was aghast at the idea of gunplay on the streets of Belfast. But as the Troubles unfolded the UVF and other loyalist groups mushroomed from tiny organisations into substantial structures with thousands of members.

In those circles Spence was venerated as a founding father of militant loyalism and a hero figure. Released on parole for his daughter's wedding in 1972, he was "kidnapped" by the UVF and remained at large for four months, adding a Scarlet Pimpernel aspect to his reputation.

As other Protestants joined him in jail he became "O/C" (officer commanding) of UVF prisoners in Long Kesh prison, where he was known as a strict disciplinarian.

Then in 1977 he sent major shock waves through the paramilitary world when, in a Twelfth of July address to UVF prisoners, he called on both loyalists and republicans to declare "a universal ceasefire" – a phrase echoed in yesterday's announcement.

He went on to say that loyalists and republicans should sit down together for talks, and to condemn "bigoted Unionist politicians". His appeals went unheeded, but although he was out of step with mainstream loyalist thinking he remained a respected figure in those quarters.

Over the years he made what were, in loyalist terms, a number of unconventional moves, resigning as UVF O/C and studying the Irish language and Irish history. Released on licence in 1984 after 18 years behind bars, he supported integrated education, described himself as a moderate socialist, and corresponded with the late Tomás Ó Fiaich, who was then head of the Catholic church in Ireland.

He associated closely with the UVF but made no secret of his continuing belief in a ceasefire. It was therefore fitting that, 17 years after he first advocated it, he should have been chosen to break the news to the world.

The general relief at the loyalist ceasefire declaration was all the greater since for several years the loyalists had actually been killing more people than the IRA.

14 OCTOBER 1994   THE INDEPENDENT

Savage killers who marked hatred in blood

Two years after the event Harry Whan, divisional ambulance officer for the city of Belfast, still finds himself reliving the horror of a loyalist gun attack on a betting shop which killed five Catholics and wounded nine others.

"The scene was horrific, with bodies everywhere," Mr Whan recalled. "In that confined space there was a smell from the gunfire and all the bleeding and whatever that you couldn't describe.

"It has an effect on you as an individual. I get flashbacks to it, I get visions of what was going on. Even now talking about it, I get flashbacks to the original scene as I walked through the door: the smell, the feeling of being there. For other ambulancemen it was worse: they were knee deep in it, dealing with the dead and dying."

What Mr Whan and his colleagues were dealing with was a tactic which has produced some of the worst excesses of the Troubles: the indiscriminate loyalist attack aimed at killing as many Catholics as possible. Northern Ireland is now clinging to the hope that it has seen the last of such incidents.

The record of the backstreet loyalist groups has been written in blood across the Troubles. Fifteen Catholics dead at McGurk's bar when the little north Belfast pub collapsed after a bombing; more than 30 killed by no-warning bombs in Dublin and Monaghan in the Republic; six dead in that bookies; hundreds more in incidents now only dimly recalled.

The IRA has received most of the attention and the publicity, but loyalist groups, principally the Ulster Volunteer Force and Ulster Defence Association, have taken around 900 lives, more than a quarter of all those killed in the Troubles.

The barbarity of some of the killings continues to cause shudders. Men shot on their doorsteps, or on their way to work, or in bed; men mown down in "spray jobs" in pubs and bookies' shops; men tortured with red-hot pokers; women beaten to death; men and women stabbed to death with inhuman savagery.

The IRA would carry out cold, often clinically calculated assassinations which its spokesmen would coolly seek to justify: a police reservist had been shot because he was part of "the British war machine"; that plumber had to die because he was carrying out maintenance work in army camps.

Some loyalist assassins tried to be cool professionals but many were of a more frightening type: unintelligent, uneducated, tattooed, and clearly full of straight sectarian hate and a thirst for revenge. Often they killed while drunk; often their victims were chosen at random; often their deaths were horrible.

Unlike republicans, many imprisoned loyalists became remorseful and disowned their actions, sometimes becoming born-again Christians. But others were sustained by the belief that force was the only answer to the IRA – that conventional politics were not sufficient to protect their interests, and had to be supplemented by assassination.

Ample historical precedents existed for the paramilitary groups. As far back as the 18th century there was a tradition of rural gangs banding together for agrarian or sectarian purposes: the Protestant Peep O' Day Boys would clash with the Catholic Defenders.

To this ancient folk memory was appended a more recent, and still applicable, political point, for Northern Ireland came into being as a direct result of a threatened revolt by Protestants in 1912. When home rule for Ireland seemed inevitable, the Protestants of the north-east organised a large and plainly illegal Ulster Volunteer Force, armed with 25,000 rifles smuggled in from Germany.

The UVF openly threatened to fight Britain in order to remain British, but the outbreak of the First World War averted open confrontation. After the war the south of Ireland broke from Britain, but Northern Ireland remained attached to it, with many Protestants concluding they had delivered themselves from the united Ireland they dreaded through the threat of force.

In a blurring of legality and illegality that has remained in the Protestant psyche, they felt themselves justified in breaking the law of the land by reference to a higher purpose, that of preserving their heritage.

When the Troubles broke out in the late 1960s many working-class loyalists saw the civil rights movement as simply the IRA in a new and more insidious guise. In the Protestant ghettos concessions to the Catholic minority were viewed as weakening Protestant rights, and the first street clashes broke out.

Earlier, in 1966, a tiny loyalist group based in a Shankill Road bar and fuelled with large amounts of alcohol, had killed three people in drunken but lethal escapades. It called itself the UVF. A number of its members were jailed, including Gusty Spence. This was the same Gusty Spence who yesterday declared: "Let us firmly resolve never again to permit our political circumstances to degenerate into bloody warfare."

At the time of these first killings most loyalists thought Spence and his gang were crazy, but after the first riots an ominous piece of graffiti appeared on the Shankill Road. It said: "Gusty was right."

At first most Protestant groups confined their activities to vigilante patrols, but as the situation deteriorated more and more contemplated the use of force to counteract the IRA's violence. By 1972 republican terrorism was rising steeply while the constitutional nationalist representatives, in particular the Social Democratic and Labour party, were making political inroads.

The abolition of the Protestant-dominated Stormont government in the spring of 1972 opened the paramilitary floodgates. Up to 40,000 Protestants joined underground groups, principally the UDA, and marched in their thousands through the streets of Belfast.

At the same moment, the killings began in the backstreets and alleyways. The IRA said it was fighting a war with Britain, but it became obvious that to the UDA every Catholic was a target. More than 100 Catholic civilians, most of them chosen at random, were killed in 1972 alone.

By 1974 the UVF had developed into a similar assassination force. In all, the loyalists have killed around 900 people. Well over 500 of these died in the five years from 1972 to 1976 as the extreme Protestants demonstrated their readiness to kill to oppose changes that would benefit nationalism.

The high point of loyalist paramilitary power came in 1974, when a UDA-inspired general strike brought large parts of Northern Ireland to a standstill and led to the collapse of a powersharing administration. But three years later the organisation overreached itself when, in concert with the Rev Ian Paisley, it attempted to stage a rerun of the stoppage. This strike ignominiously fizzled out, dealing a body blow to the credibility of the paramilitaries.

That credibility suffered further blows as it became apparent that important loyalist figures had become involved in racketeering and criminality on a major scale. The killing of one of the chief racketeers, Jim Craig, in an internal UDA feud did little to lift this stain from the paramilitary image.

The late 1970s and early 1980s were in any event a time of contraction for the paramilitary groups, as the general Protestant population came to feel less insecure. After 1976 the British Labour administration took a tougher law and order line, the fortunes of the IRA seemed to be fading, and consequently fewer Protestants saw the point of active paramilitarism.

As a result both membership and the killing rate fell away sharply. For a time deaths averaged only around a dozen a year, but the mid and late 1980s brought an IRA revival and the perception that nationalists were making political gains through the Anglo-Irish agreement. This brought an upsurge which has resulted in a loyalist killing rate of around 40 victims annually since 1991, for the first time ever actually overtaking the death toll of the IRA.

The loyalist ceasefire therefore goes sharply against the trend of recent years, for it has become clear that there is no shortage of support and toleration for their activities, and certainly no shortage of recruits.

Unemployment is high in many of the most hardline Protestant areas, such as the Shankill Road. Many youths in these districts have clearly felt they have no stake in society and nothing to lose by becoming involved in violence; and there has certainly been a widespread feeling that violence pays and gets results.

A year ago a senior Presbyterian churchman said privately: "I'm afraid there is a growing toleration of violence within the Unionist community. The view is that democratic politics doesn't work, that political negotiation doesn't get anywhere, and the only thing the powers-that-be understand is violence.

"Young people feel they have nothing to lose – they have no stake in society, no motivation. That vacuum is being filled by the paramilitaries, who give them an alleged cause, a purpose for living."

Paramilitary loyalism is more splintered than the IRA, being less centralised and more based on strong local personalities who run their own areas. The question will therefore arise of whether all the different elements and districts will accept the ceasefire: the coming weeks and months will show whether it is to be universally accepted.

The culture of paramilitarism has centuries-old roots within Northern Ireland society, and the experience of the last quarter of a century means that many youths and men have grown up in ghettos where organised armed groups are a daily fact of life.

Those groups are not about to disappear: rather, they will find modified roles for themselves within working-class loyalism. This will doubtless mean that many of their illegalities will continue for the foreseeable future: the hope, however, is that the wholesale slaughter is over.

The loyalist community is known for its volatility, but this period saw swings of unusual magnitude. While some Unionists continued to express fear and suspicion of the IRA ceasefire, other elements spoke of a new start and the need for dialogue. Even more surprisingly, some of the most progressive noises came from hardline districts, in particular the Shankill Road, where an IRA bomb had killed nine local people a year previously.

Ulstermen march
to a new drum

Exactly 20 years ago, in October 1974, Billy Hutchinson, a young man from the Shankill Road, Belfast's loyalist heartland, acted as getaway driver for a loyalist gang which shot dead two Catholic men on the neighbouring Falls Road.

A year later Hutchinson, a member of the junior wing of the Ulster Volunteer Force, was sentenced to life imprisonment for his part in the killings. After a difficult start in prison he settled down, took a degree in town planning and did some thinking.

Today he is one of more than 250 men, both loyalist and republican, who have been freed on licence after serving life sentences: most of them, like him, were convicted for murder. He now devotes himself to community development work on the Shankill Road. Having served 15 years behind bars, he is anti-violence: as the loyalist ceasefire was declared he hovered at the back of the hall, a large smile on his face.

At a conference on Protestant identity on the Shankill Road earlier this month, Hutchinson picked a quarrel with Mrs Iris Robinson, wife of Peter Robinson MP, who is deputy leader of the Rev Ian Paisley's Democratic Unionist party. It was an exchange which laid bare the tensions that exist within loyalism between the would-be modernisers, who believe they need to react creatively to the momentous events sweeping Northern Ireland, and the traditionalists.

Mrs Robinson had just told the crowded conference that Mr Paisley would not sit down with Sinn Féin. Mr Hutchinson and his associates believe that at some stage this will have to happen. She declared: "It would be akin to asking Myra Hindley to sit down and develop a document on child care. Why should Mr Paisley sit down with Gerry Adams, who has the blood of so many hundreds of people on his hands?"

Hutchinson, an intense fair-haired man now in his late 30s, challenged her. "She's sitting there saying you can't talk to murderers, but here on the Shankill Road thousands of young men and women have been to prison for fighting the IRA and republicanism. Now she's calling these people murderers."

Mrs Robinson replied: "As a born-again Christian I cannot support anyone who murders. That has always been my stand." "Then why do you keep saying that there's going to be a civil war?" asked Mr Hutchinson. "Because you read the writing on the wall," came her response.

Hutchinson called out: "You and your husband and your party have cried to the people out there to get out on the streets and fight republicanism. You can't deny them now, you have to stand by them."

"No," said Mrs Robinson. "I say you use your numbers to fight through the ballot box. I've never asked anyone to come on the streets." Hutchinson, referring to the days when Mr Paisley and Mr Robinson took to the streets in recruitment rallies for a shadowy organisation, Ulster Resistance, responded: "When you wear red berets and march in ranks it's a statement of militarism, and you scare the life out of young men who then think they have to go out and fight. This is hypocrisy." Mrs Robinson was clearly shaken by the force of the spirited confrontation.

The exchange was one of a number of heated moments at the conference, which was itself a sign that a community not given to introspection is finally asking searching questions about itself. Protestants and Unionists have traditionally taken refuge in the past: the community's comforting buzzwords include tradition, birthright and heritage. But now, in the post-IRA-ceasefire world, at least some are re-examining that heritage, and contemplating the future with a mixture of nervousness and hope. And some of the most radical new ideas are coming from Billy Hutchinson and other politicised ex-prisoners, once members of the illegal UVF, who now say they want to keep the next generation of Shankill Road teenagers out of jail.

There are still, however, a great many who prefer the old ways. The little bookstall outside the hall, run by a member of Mr Paisley's party, offered for sale *Murder in the Vatican – America, Russia and Papal Plots*, and *The Secret History of the Jesuits*, which proclaimed: "The Roman Catholic Institution is not a Christian Church and never was. Prophetically she is the whore of Revelation." *The Loyalist Song Book*, on sale at £2, offered a series of ditties to gladden the most sectarian heart. "Oh give me a home where there's no Pope of Rome", sung to the tune of "Home on the Range", has the chorus:

> No, no Pope of Rome,
> No chapels to sadden my eyes,
> No nuns and no priests and no rosary beads,
> And every day is the Twelfth of July.

But inside the hall another UVF ex-prisoner, David Ervine, is singing a different tune. "The politics of division see thousands of people dead, most of them working class, and headstones on the graves of young men. We have been fools:

let's not be fools any longer. All elements must be comfortable within Northern Ireland. We have got to extend the hand of friendship, we have got to take the peacelines down brick by brick, and somehow or other we have got to introduce class politics. You can't eat a flag.

"Unionism, I believe, has got lost against a background of violence, which was preceded by a background of patronage and suppression. Edward Carson said, 'Look after the minority.' We didn't − and have we suffered for it. We have got to appeal to the Catholic, because Catholics, at least some of them, have shown their willingness to be Unionist. Unionism is a wholly legitimate philosophy which has the right to be heard, but we have found ourselves friendless. We're going to have to be honourable with each other's aspirations. That means I will concede, not my nationality, but my friendship." Twenty years ago people who said that sort of thing were denounced as traitors and Lundies and hounded out of loyalist politics, but Ervine received a warm round of applause.

The conference was not, however, a clear triumph for this new avowedly non-sectarian, left-leaning loyalism. Rather, it heard a medley of old and new ideas. The Rev Ian Paisley, who delivered a brief speech and then left, railed in traditional fashion against "the dogmas of Rome and the jackboot of Vaticanism". His way forward was not at all couched in political terms: "We need a revival of our Protestantism, we need a revival of our religion. We all need a spiritual awakening, a return to the basics."

John Taylor MP of the Ulster Unionists, the largest Protestant party, concentrated on economics: "In a united Ireland the three and a half million people in the south would have to send us £1,000 per man, woman and child each year to maintain our present level of services," he declared. Like Mr Paisley, he eschewed the rhetoric of reconciliation: "I'm an Ulsterman, not an Irishman. I don't jig at crossroads or play Gaelic football or speak Irish. We've got two races on this island. In every respect we are a different race from Gerry Adams. We are not fellow Irishmen."

The man from the Orange Order, Fraser Agnew, was even more upfront and direct. Orangeism had been accused of dividing the Protestant and Catholic working classes and keeping them apart, he said. "But is that a bad thing?" he asked. "If it ensures that the freedoms won through the Glorious Revolution remain intact, then it's no bad thing," he concluded.

The approaches on offer from Mr Taylor, Mr Paisley and Mr Agnew are precisely what the ex-prisoners are trying to get away from. They seek to make a new start, but the precedents for success are not bright. The history of Unionist politics is littered with breakaway parties and individuals who make an initial impact but later contract into minor niches. Many Unionists and loyalists grumble about their traditional leaders, but in the privacy of the ballot box find their pens moving, however reluctantly, towards the familiar old names.

The emergence of more progressive forces depends on the proposition that peace will create new possibilities and release new energies. The question is whether the ending of violence will now create new space for a new philosophy which seeks to find common ground, and which has learnt that a politics which dwells on divisions can lead first to the gun and then the prison cell.

By contrast with the Shankill radicals, mainstream Unionist representatives were less enthusiastic about the prospect of change.

17 OCTOBER 1994   THE INDEPENDENT

Unionists adjusting to new political landscape

Inside the Ulster Unionist party's annual conference the grassroots sat listening to dire warnings that the IRA was not finished yet and that a resumption of republican violence could be on the cards.

But outside the inn at Carrickfergus, Co Antrim, the level of security gave an indication of the army and police assessment of the threat level: for much of the day there were no troops and no police officers in sight.

Normally, political conferences in Northern Ireland are ringed with armoured Land Rovers as armed police check cars on the way in; but now things have changed. Inside the well-attended conference, this cautious, conservative, elderly party – "we're very much a blue rinse set-up," one representative admitted – was beginning to adjust to the recent dramatic changes.

The feel-good factor was palpable in the hall, with much praise and much

41

genuine affection for James Molyneaux, who is seen as a low-key but effective leader. A senior party member said privately: "Generally, they feel that Jim's doing a good job and that he has a very good relationship with John Major. They like the feeling of having influence at court."

Many speakers were critical of the Rev Ian Paisley's Democratic Unionist party, accusing it of scaremongering and groundlessly whipping up grassroots concerns. One councillor declared: "The greatest danger we face is self-destruction through these negative tactics. This exploitation of sectarian fears, the whining and the whingeing, take a toll on the Unionist spirit." The party leadership's position, in contrast to Mr Paisley's, was summed up by Ken Maginnis MP: "The union has been threatened. The union is now safe."

Only a few Young Turks thought Mr Molyneaux should be extracting more from his relationship with Mr Major. "The next two years is the time to capitalise on our influence," said David Burnside, formerly of British Airways. Another speaker said of the Conservative government: "We must continue to keep pressure on them. Fortunately their majority is weak – hopefully they may be in difficulties over the Post Office and other issues. It's up to Unionists to keep the pressure on to ensure that they have some backbone."

After the Young Turks came a surprising Old Turk, Enoch Powell, who in his 80s is venerated as a party elder statesman. Mr Powell was given two standing ovations despite the fact that he took the very opposite of the Molyneaux line: this was a time of the greatest possible danger for Northern Ireland, he warned, since the British government was operating to a game plan first to give them self-government and then to bring them to a united Ireland. They must hold fast to "the union, the whole union and nothing but the union".

Delegates were deeply cynical of the peace process: there was a stream of sarcastic references to "Saint John" Hume, and numerous predictions that the IRA would start up again, possibly in January 1995.

This is a staid party, which ideally prefers political movement to come slowly and gently. But the new atmosphere has not left it untouched: senior members were for instance saying privately that there will at some stage be contact with Sinn Féin. "It'll not be before Christmas," said one quite casually, demonstrating that new ideas and approaches may be permeating the most unexpected of places.

In one part of the political landscape, however, the ceasefires left old certainties and attitudes untouched.

Paisley denounces all sides in peace process

The Rev Ian Paisley made it clear to his Democratic Unionist party's annual conference that his response to the peace process is to take a harder line than ever. The DUP leader told the faithful in Dungannon, Co Tyrone, that the IRA cessation was a con, he promised to wreck any assembly emerging from the talks process, and characterised the Ulster Unionists as being fooled by a treacherous John Major.

In a speech marked by denunciations of the British government, the Ulster Unionist party, the Irish Republic and above all the Catholic church, Mr Paisley declared that Protestants faced "the worst crisis in Ulster's history since the setting up of the state".

His entire approach was at odds with the thesis of optimists who point out that the killings have almost stopped and look forward to a new and more peaceful era. This has led to a perceived marginalisation of Mr Paisley as a Jeremiah out of step with the thrust of new developments. But the party conference had one of its best-ever attendances, with 500 or more members giving him a most rousing reception.

He announced a new initiative aimed at focusing attention on Unionist consent. This may take the form of legal action aimed at proving that the Downing Street declaration is at odds with the Act of Union of 1801.

The climax of his speech came when he declared: "Are we going to agree to a partnership with the IRA men of blood who have slain our loved ones, destroyed our country, burnt our churches, tortured our people and now demand that we should become slaves in a country fit only for nuns' men and monks' women to live in?

"We cannot bow the knee to these traitors in Whitehall, nor to those offspring of the Vatican who walk the corrupted corridors of power in Dublin, in Europe and in Washington. In the propaganda war we must excel, answering the lies with truth, and smoking out from their lairs the media skunks, cleansing their putrid odour from the face of Ulster's earth."

Mr Paisley is clearly concerned to wrest some of the initiative back from James

Molyneaux's Ulster Unionist party, which is now seen to have the ear of a British government anxious for its support in crucial Commons votes. Mr Molyneaux has given general approval for Mr Major's handling of the peace process, arguing that the union with Britain is safe and that Unionist interests are being looked after by Mr Major.

The Paisleyite projection is precisely the opposite, portraying Mr Molyneaux as the puppet and poodle of a government intent on "the monstrous act of the final betrayal of the union". The DUP, as a party which thrives on conflict and crisis, is clearly uneasy about the possibility of a new and more settled political environment. Its fortunes will depend on whether Mr Paisley's message of dangers, or Mr Molyneaux's calmness, is borne out by events.

For the rest, it was vintage Paisley. He described the Republic as backward, superstitious and priest-ridden; SDLP leader John Hume as an inveterate hater of the union; the Downing Street declaration as Jesuitical; Mr Major as bribing and appeasing the IRA; President Clinton as the Whitewater crook; and the Pope as the Anti-Christ.

Mr Paisley's son, Ian Jnr, and his deputy, Peter Robinson, missed the conference since they were in South Africa studying how politicians there had reacted to a radically changed situation. The message from Dungannon on Saturday, however, was that this was a time not of opportunity but of peril, a time for remaining steadfast. Mr Paisley's party, as one speaker put it, "is like the old Orange flute – you can scrub it and treat it with holy water but it always plays the same old tune".

Within weeks of the IRA cessation many nationalist elements had become openly critical of what they characterised as the British government's overcautious response to the ceasefire.

One source close to the Irish government said Dublin believed the IRA had stopped its campaign for good, but added: "It would be very difficult for them to start again – except in one circumstance, and that is if effectively the British are using this to pursue a Unionist agenda. If they do, it's almost inevitable that you'd get a new cycle of violence."

The south, by contrast, attempted to move the process ahead with all speed. In the Downing Street declaration Albert Reynolds had promised to bring Sinn Féin into the Republic's political processes, and in late October an important step was taken to effect this.

29 OCTOBER 1994   THE INDEPENDENT

South brings republicans in from the cold

The most important function of the Forum for Peace and Reconciliation, which met for the first time in Dublin yesterday, is to help bring the republican movement into Irish constitutional politics.

While John Major has insisted on playing a slow and cautious game with Sinn Féin, Albert Reynolds has seen his role as moving briskly to seize the moment and, as quickly as possible, bring the republicans in from the cold.

The IRA cessation of violence was announced on 31 August; the historic handshake between Mr Reynolds and Gerry Adams took place on 6 September; and yesterday Sinn Féin got its feet under the political table in Dublin.

Mr Major, by contrast, has not yet authorised any contact with Sinn Féin: his timetable is that the first exploratory contact between officials and republicans will take place "before this year is out".

The genesis of the forum lay in an originally much more grandiose idea, with the notion of an all-inclusive conference table which might even produce a binding report. That early idea has contracted considerably, and yesterday's proceedings opened without participation from any of the major northern Unionist groupings. But it still, in Dublin's eyes, has a significant part to play in the peace process.

Mr Reynolds's theory is that it is worth taking risks in forcing the pace if the result is that Sinn Féin becomes inextricably bound up in the political processes. One school of thought in Dublin has it that he is moving altogether too quickly, while another view is that Mr Major is proceeding too slowly.

One sign of this was Dublin's displeasure at London's decision to have the British ambassador, David Blatherwick, stay away from the forum's inaugural meeting because of the presence of a Sinn Féin delegation.

The forum's terms of reference set out that it is to examine ways to establish peace, stability and reconciliation, and to remove barriers of distrust. As of now there exists next to no trust between republicans and conventional southern politicians.

Sinn Féin gets less than 2 per cent of the vote in the Irish Republic, and for many years has stood no chance of winning a Dáil seat. Most mainstream southern politicians have never met Gerry Adams or indeed any of Sinn Féin's leadership: nearly all of them detest what they believe he used to stand for, which is the use of violence.

The general hope is that the forum will assist in gradually breaking down these barriers of distrust. Unionist parties have characterised it as essentially a nationalist exercise, and declined to take part. There will, however, be some non-nationalist input from the middle-of-the-road Alliance party, which in Northern Ireland takes votes from both communities.

The forum's chairwoman, Catherine McGuinness, is a southern Protestant with a northern background who was recently appointed as a judge. She has been a campaigner for women's rights and a prominent member of the Church of Ireland synod.

The ceasefires brought a fundamental reassessment of economic prospects. One key figure was distinctly optimistic about the future.

Leading businessman sees great potential for economy

The prospect of peace has given Northern Ireland its brightest economic outlook for a quarter of a century, according to one of the key figures in Belfast's business and financial world.

Peace will, in the view of Sir George Quigley, bring in new difficulties, but, overall, Northern Ireland is well placed to take advantage of the opportunities thrown up at this historic juncture.

He sees an economy surprisingly well positioned for the new era, with much entrepreneurial spirit already evident in little-known but healthy medium-sized companies, and with significant attractions to offer potential new investors.

According to Sir George: "When you talk to business people they're in a very buoyant mood – surprisingly bullish, not a lot of pessimism around. I think when everybody's preoccupations with security are taken away then you will find a lot of potential, a lot of dormant, latent potential will be released."

He is a pivotal figure in the local economy. Following a civil service career in charge of Northern Ireland finances, he is involved in many of Belfast's biggest concerns: chairman of the Ulster Bank, chairman of the Royal group of hospitals [he resigned in January 1996] and a director of Shorts aircraft company.

Of the ending of violence he says: "There are clear benefits to arise from a prolonged period of stability. These include greater inward investment, the potential in tourism, the many benefits that could arise from more cross-border economic co-operation and, perhaps most important of all, the political stability that peace would provide for general economic activity.

"When you get a peaceful environment you get the generation of much greater confidence, people are able to plan ahead, to take more ambitious decisions. It would be more conducive to a more dynamic, outward-looking enterprise and industrial base. The combination of economic recovery and the benefits that could arise from a period of peace provides an economic scenario that I believe has never been bettered in the last 25 years."

The standard view of the Northern Ireland economy is that a quarter-century

47

of violence and instability has left it in a parlous state, with a huge public sector, a weak private sector, and a dependence on Britain for money – the subvention currently runs at well over £3 billion annually.

Unemployment is high and there is said to be a lack of entrepreneurial skills. Furthermore, it is claimed, the ending of the republican and loyalist terrorist campaigns will mean longer dole queues as the gradual dismantling of the security apparatus puts tens of thousands of police officers and others out of work.

The loss of security jobs will, he admits, pose short-term problems. He says: "If peace and political stability can be achieved and sustained in the longer term, obviously substantial numbers of people employed in the security forces and security-related jobs will be adversely affected. But to argue that peace will bring more problems than benefits is perverse. Clearly, there will be downside effects in the short term, but what's important is that the adjustment problems are dealt with carefully and sensitively."

The major problem area on which he believes attention should be focused is that of the long-term unemployed: Northern Ireland has around 55,000 people who have been without a job for more than 12 months. Many of these are concentrated in the grim black spots where male unemployment can reach 60 per cent. Clearly, it is no coincidence that these are areas, such as the Shankill and the Falls, which have also been the seedbeds of paramilitarism.

According to Sir George: "The risk is that you may get more economic activity, but then find the bulk of jobs are still being taken by people who have been relatively recently associated with the labour market. Something needs to be done to target the long-term unemployed directly and to reconnect them with the world of work. That's a very important factor for political stability. If you don't get some action on the long-term unemployed, you could in fact have an increasing gap between those in work and those out of it. That is not a basis for a stable society."

Although Sir George did not spell it out in religious terms, two of the goals ahead are finding new jobs for people from the security sector, most of whom are Protestant, and helping the long-term jobless, many of whom are Catholic. These are formidable tasks, but he believes there is a largely unappreciated underlying strength in local firms, and much local talent around.

"We have got a fairly dense texture of small- to medium-size companies, about some of whom the community at large knows very little. Because of the Troubles they've been carrying on doing the job but they haven't got a lot of profile," he says.

"Their management has been tested very severely in the last 25 years. I think they have come through very well indeed. It is those companies that are the engines of growth, and I think there's a very good base.

"There's much more of an enterprise culture around than people generally acknowledge – not just in the business sector but also in the voluntary and community sector. If those people were in the commercial profit-oriented area they would be superb."

His view of the future is upbeat but, in common with almost all local political parties, trade unions and business figures, his optimism is based on the belief that all or most of the "peace dividend" will remain in Northern Ireland rather than reverting to the Treasury.

He insists: "We should be very careful about taking a quick peace dividend in terms of reduced public expenditure. We want to be careful that we don't destabilise things. Hopefully as we build a stronger private sector the need for a high level of public spending will diminish, but unfortunately we're not at that point yet. There's bound to be a temptation to try to pare off 100 or 200 million pounds, but in this instance if we take the medium- to long-term view, we could gain enormously from that expenditure."

He does not, however, argue that all responsibility rests with the British government. Political progress is critically important, he says: "We need very broad-based involvement of the whole community in this effort. In the last analysis any society which has made a go of its economy has very strong political institutions which have been able to articulate values, set objectives and mobilise ambition within the community. One shouldn't underestimate the value of that as an ingredient for success."

November brought serious problems for the peace process. First came a murder, with a 53-year-old postal worker, Frank Kerr, shot dead by an IRA gang during an armed robbery in Newry, Co Down. The republican ceasefire was thrown into doubt but the IRA leadership issued a statement saying it had not sanctioned the robbery and had granted no one permission to use arms.

Next came political disruption when the coalition government, led by Albert Reynolds, ran into trouble. His administration suddenly became caught up in an imbroglio concerning a paedophile priest, Father Brendan Smyth, and the Irish Labour party, led by Dick Spring, pulled out of the coalition.

It brought to a sudden end the career of Reynolds, a politician who had been closely identified with the peace process. Domestically, he will be remembered as the man who brought down two of his own governments and lost an election. Historically, however, he stands a realistic chance of having a place in history as one of the men who brought lasting peace to Ireland.

Since he had played a leading part in the peace process, there were initial fears that his departure might pose a real danger to the ceasefires. Surprisingly quickly, however, the Republic concluded that its domestic turbulence would not impact on the peace process.

Peace: rock amid a sea of trouble?

The Dublin daily papers have contained scarcely a word about whether the fall of Albert Reynolds's government might or might not disrupt the Irish peace process. This is partly because the Irish Republic is engrossed in its own domestic affairs, but more importantly because a consensus has emerged throughout the state that the process looks robust enough to withstand this type of buffeting.

Only 12 weeks after the IRA cessation of violence that process has become an established, even integral, part of the Irish scene. But at the height of the crisis, politicians of all parties suspended their dispute and trooped off to the scheduled meeting of the Forum for Peace and Reconciliation, there to meet and mingle with Sinn Féin.

The process is considered so strong and so safe because public opinion throughout the Republic considers it to be such a patently obvious good thing. Since the IRA ceasefire was announced two people have died, one killed by loyalists and another by republicans. In the same period last year there were 34 killings: already, then, the feeling is that there has been a peace dividend purely in terms of lives saved. The general sense is also that both republicans and loyalists seem sincere when they say they have no intentions of returning to violence.

There is no certainty as to what the next Irish government will look like, but whatever its complexion, support for the peace process is so nearly universal that no new administration would be forgiven for placing it in jeopardy. Earlier in the week some worries were voiced about the effect of the political crisis on the process, but these faded as a general judgement took shape that no real threat to it existed.

Reassurance was also drawn from the hasty readjustments some politicians were seen to make to their positions. Fine Gael leader John Bruton, for example, was one of the process's most exacting scrutineers but is now emphasising that it would be safe with him. When Mr Reynolds resigned, Mr Bruton was on his feet in the Dáil within minutes with a plaintive little declaration: "I have had to ask him difficult questions but I hope he understands that is my job, and I do so in order to ensure that the peace process may be more durable, having been tested more carefully."

For a southern politician, Mr Bruton is unusually sympathetic to northern Unionism – Albert Reynolds once referred to him as "John Unionist". Northern republicans have already signalled that a Bruton-led administration, which would inevitably include some other ferociously anti-republican parties, is their idea of a cabinet from hell.

Such a government would not set out to derail the peace process, but it is questionable whether it would pull out all the stops, as did Mr Reynolds, to make things as easy as possible for the republican movement. Nonetheless, the general southern view is that the process would be secure enough with Bruton. If he does not get to be Taoiseach it will not be because of the peace process but because of other issues, such as his economic views and his general temperament and competence.

But while Dublin opinion may be basically content on the peace issue, it all looks (as so often) very different from a northern perspective. To begin with, Unionist opinion still contains strong elements of suspicion and worry: suspicion, for example, that the whole process is designed to do down Unionism, and worry that peace could bring penalties by costing Protestants jobs in security and other fields.

On the northern nationalist side, there is a continuing anxiety about just how hardy a plant the peace process actually is, and concern that an Irish government without Albert Reynolds would not put the same effort into nurturing it.

Viewed from this perspective, the process has settled into a familiar Anglo-Irish pattern – the British government does move, but always more slowly than nationalists would like, and usually after a great deal of pressure from Dublin. If the next Irish government eases off, then London could relax and the process could come under new strains. Reaching a judgement on whether this scenario would actually endanger peace is difficult, since so much depends on the internal workings of the ultra-secret republican movement.

There seems to have been IRA involvement in the armed robbery which led to the killing of a postal worker in Newry, Co Down. If there was, no one is clear whether this represents a challenge to the cessation by dissident members. If the IRA should decide at some point to return to violence, it seems inevitable that Gerry Adams, Martin McGuinness and practically all the other leaders of Sinn Féin would be swept aside, for they are intimately identified with the cessation policy.

Sinn Féin's recent gains, including its new political access in Dublin, London and the US, would be instantly reversed. Shorn of its new-found political status, it would be reverting to the brutally simple, and most unpromising, theory that terrorism alone can achieve its aims. There could be a split which would be devastating for the movement. These facts militate against a renewed campaign.

So too does the overall mood in the north. The IRA and loyalist cessations evoked a mixture of emotions, but the prevailing sentiment, in both communities, was one of sheer, blessed relief. That alone gives grounds for optimism that the ceasefires will stick. But even with these powerful forces at work, nothing can be taken for granted in a country with such a history of violence. Both London and whichever new Dublin government emerges will need careful management and delicate judgement to ensure that peace is preserved.

POSTSCRIPT

John Bruton and Dick Spring eventually did a deal and formed a new coalition government in December 1994.

The peace process attracted much international interest and good will. In December, for example, the European Commission announced an aid package worth £231 million to help those areas most severely affected by the Troubles.

In the United States the Clinton administration maintained a close interest in the peace process, but Anglo-American relations were in fragile condition after Washington allowed Gerry Adams into the States. New strains appeared when John Major announced plans for a large-scale investment conference in Belfast, the government being forced to turn a somersault.

Conference rethink shows pressure on peace process

A chronicle of the last few days of frenetic cross-Atlantic activity illustrates a number of the key features of the Irish peace process. One is the government's difficulties in micro-managing the process; another is the success of Irish nationalism in internationalising the issue; and a third is the strength of the Irish-American lobby.

These elements have just combined to produce abrupt government U-turns on the question of the pace of the peace process, and in particular the issue of whether Sinn Féin should be allowed to attend this month's major investment conference in Belfast.

The idea of a conference to attract new investment to Northern Ireland was announced by John Major in October. The venture was warmly welcomed, but it has recently emerged that behind the scenes the announcement created much ill feeling in both Washington and Dublin.

This was because the three governments had been actively considering holding such a conference in the US, on a cross-border basis. Mr Major's announcement was therefore seen as an attempt to pre-empt this and to confine the exercise to Northern Ireland alone. This background was not widely known, however, and it was only this week that the conference became the subject of open public controversy. This arose when it emerged that Sinn Féin was to be excluded from its proceedings, which are to take place on 13 and 14 December.

On the morning of Wednesday 30 November the Northern Ireland Secretary, Sir Patrick Mayhew, told reporters in Belfast that it would be premature to invite Sinn Féin to the conference, since talks aimed at bringing the party into the political processes were not to begin until later in December. He added: "It's very important to maintain confidence that undue concessions are not being made to people who have, for a very long time, given their support to those who have been knocking down Belfast and destroying it."

But on Wednesday afternoon Sir Patrick's deputy, Sir John Wheeler, projected a different message when he spoke of the Sinn Féin talks opening within a few days. Asked for clarification, NIO press sources indicated that Sir Patrick's was the correct version.

54

By that point it was already clear that the exclusion of Sinn Féin had caused what one observer described as a "firestorm" in Washington and Irish-America. The rise of Irish-Americans to top-level positions in business, commerce, and politics means the issue is high on the White House agenda.

The transatlantic telephone lines were busy as Gerry Adams, SDLP leader John Hume and the Dublin government made their feelings known about the exclusion. But the American reaction to the news was already, according to the *Irish Times*, one of incredulity, dismay and anger at the decision.

The Clinton administration was already committed to sending the US Commerce Secretary, Ron Brown, to Belfast at the head of a large delegation. The general American view is that the peace process is concerned with drawing Sinn Féin into the political processes, and the exclusion of the party seemed to go directly against this philosophy.

It was shortly after 10 a.m. on 1 December that word was spread by government sources of a hurried overnight rethink, and in the afternoon Sir Patrick told the Commons that Sinn Féin members would be invited – not as party members but as representatives of local councils.

It had already been confirmed that the first government meeting with Sinn Féin was being advanced from the second half of the month to 7 December. This decision was made necessary by Sir Patrick's comments that it would be premature to have republicans at the conference before they were in talks with the government.

The episode demonstrated that, while the peace process is primarily in London's hands, other important elements will have a major say in how it is to be conducted. It also demonstrated that the government is showing an uncertain touch in its handling of the process.

Sinn Féin eventually got to go to the conference. They also got to go somewhere else – Stormont buildings, the one-time seat of Unionist government, for their first open talks with government representatives.

Sinn Féin displays
new suits and roots

A defiantly battered black taxi and a geriatric Ford Granada yesterday chugged up the half-mile hill to Stormont buildings to deliver Martin McGuinness to the heart of the British establishment.

The slightly dilapidated mode of transport projected a different message from the sartorial style of Mr McGuinness and his four republican comrades, for they emerged dressed in their Sunday best. The flinty Londonderry republican was resplendent in dapper blue blazer and grey slacks; Sean McManus, whose IRA son was shot dead by a member of the security forces he was trying to kill, wore a double-breasted grey suit.

Gerry Kelly, sentenced to life imprisonment for blowing up the Old Bailey, sported gold-rimmed glasses and a natty black briefcase secured with a combination lock. Mr Kelly is a member of the IRA army council, according to unconfirmed reports: his eventful republican career has included escaping from the Maze prison in the mass IRA break-out of 1983. A third member of the team, Siobhán O'Hanlon, has been alleged in some newspapers to have been involved in the 1988 IRA operation to place a bomb in Gibraltar which ended when the SAS shot dead three IRA members. She wore a neat business suit.

The clothes told the world that these were people of high self-esteem, striding confidently into talks with every expectation of eventual success. The old taxi, its front numberplate slightly askew and a rear hubcap missing, may have been designed to reassure the folks back home that they have not lost touch with their roots.

The incongruity between the good suits and the old bangers reflected the general confusion and perplexity about what Sinn Féin expects from the whole exercise. It is difficult to believe that they think the British will suddenly surrender and start pulling out of Northern Ireland.

On the other side of the coin is the British insistence on a hand-over of IRA arms. The IRA has called a cessation of violence, but it has disengaged from the armed struggle, not surrendered. Unilateral disarmament by the IRA would be a sign of capitulation, and the republicans have not capitulated.

There was no welcome at the door of Stormont for Mr McGuinness and his colleagues, but after a self-assured photo opportunity on the doorstep they went inside. The meeting took place in the massively overmajestic buildings which were for half a century the seat of Unionist one-party rule, and thus the symbol of nationalist exclusion from power and influence. In the last quarter-century it has been the scene of so many failed political initiatives that for many it has become an icon of the apparent futility of talking.

But both sides emerged with the message that there is business to be done between them, and more meetings are to come. The republicans deliberately emerged from the front of the building so the cameras would picture them framed against Stormont's massive granite columns. The old system of ascendancy once symbolised by the building has gone. The talking has begun, but the shape of some new system which might for the first time pre-empt violence and offer something for everyone, has yet to emerge. In the meantime one encouraging little sign could be seen in the back seat of the black taxi which waited to take Mr McGuinness and the others back home. It was a little book entitled *Finding Peace Within*.

The year ended on a note of uncertainty mixed with hope. The republicans had been accepted into nationalist politics and had begun to talk to the British government.

Billy Hutchinson, David Ervine and other loyalists formed themselves into two new parties – the Progressive Unionist party, which spoke for the Ulster Volunteer Force, and the Ulster Democratic party, speaking for the Ulster Defence Association. They too made the journey to Stormont for talks with British officials.

In Dublin John Bruton was elected Taoiseach in succession to Albert

Reynolds in mid-December. This was
greeted with some dismay by republicans,
who had come to rely heavily on
Mr Reynolds to promote their point
of view.

No one was taking peace for granted:
the Chief Constable of the RUC, Sir Hugh
Annesley, said in December that he
believed the IRA ceasefire had "a 60–40
chance" of lasting until Easter. As the
year closed, however, hopes were high
that the peace would last.

---

26 DECEMBER 1994   THE INDEPENDENT

The year
the guns fell silent

It's too much, and too soon, to call it a miracle, because in a land so steeped in conflict and paramilitarism no one can say with complete assurance that the violence will not break out again: you can never say never.

But it was a historic time for Ireland, the year when the guns fell silent. With so many uncertainties still in the air, northern Irish prudence and caution has not yet given way to celebration: fingers are still crossed, guards have not yet been fully dropped. Yet there has already been a partial transformation. North Belfast ghetto Catholics have stopped glancing nervously at cars which might contain loyalist gunmen; now they wonder if jobs might some day come their way.

Policemen have stopped looking under their cars each morning for IRA Semtex boobytraps. Life is safer for them, but now they worry whether lasting peace means their jobs will go. The mood of Belfast has changed as shoppers who for two decades stayed away because of the car bombs now clog up the city streets. It has been the city's best Christmas for decades.

Now republican and loyalist hard men, togged out in double-breasted suits, are trooping up to Stormont buildings in Belfast to talk to senior government officials about guns, demilitarisation and, eventually, Northern Ireland's future. In the 1970s one of those republicans was given a life sentence for setting off car bombs in London. In the 1970s one of those loyalists stabbed to death a nationalist politician and his woman companion, later penitently explaining to a judge: "I could see the IRA taking over Ulster and I was against this. I thought if I killed Roman Catholics it would stop them."

That was then, this is now. Both those men have spent long years in prison, and both are now trying out dialogue rather than violence. The unanswered question hangs in the air: how can the aspirations of loyalists, who want closer ties with Britain, be reconciled with those of republicans, who want to sever the British link? No answer is yet apparent, but the fact they are talking rather than killing is a source of hope.

There seemed little hope late last year, when a wave of violence plunged Northern Ireland into one of its darkest-ever periods. An IRA bombing which went wrong killed one of the bombers and nine Protestants. Loyalists took their revenge by killing 13 Catholics.

The mood of dread at that time was described in a report from the *Independent*: "Belfast is a city numbed with the shock of too many killings, a city braced for the near-inevitability of more deaths, a city wondering fearfully what fresh horrors lie in store. Two more deaths mean that 14 people have been killed and more than 60 injured in four days. Yesterday brought yet more images of pathos and horror. A little white coffin bore a seven-year-old girl to her grave, followed by the coffins of her mother and father. At another scene of death the hysterical daughter of a murdered pensioner sobbed in the street. At a refuse depot the body of a council worker had been removed, leaving behind a packet of Silk Cut cigarettes and a puddle of his fresh blood. Strewn all around the yard were dozens of empty bullet cases – Belfast confetti."

The contrast with the Christmas just past could not be more striking: in little more than 12 months Belfast has gone from blackness to hope as, against all the odds, the peace process re-emerged and eventually produced results. The whole process has been characterised by uncertainty about what exactly goes on within the republican movement, and little enough is known of the exact state of play within it. It is conceivable that disgruntled elements could break away, or attempt to force a change of mind on the leadership, or indeed attempt to replace it.

It is impossible to be entirely confident that the campaigns of violence are over for ever. It is a fair bet, in fact, that if the government were to simply ride roughshod over the republicans, the campaign would probably start again. Exactly the same holds true for the loyalists: if they feel their essential interests are threatened, then their ceasefire could crumble.

But each passing week without killings makes a full-scale resumption of the conflict more difficult to imagine. If the ceasefires do hold, then ahead lie not months but years of trying to construct a political settlement. This will be fraught with difficulties, but historic and unprecedented steps towards that goal were taken in 1994, and the continuation of peace should make that task much easier. It was the year that showed that faith, courage and perseverance, even in the darkest of days, can overcome despair. The people of Northern Ireland are having a taste of peace, are relishing it, and will not treat kindly anyone who places it in jeopardy.

The new year opened with more signs that a gradual demilitarisation process was under way. Twenty-five years and five months after the first nervous British tommies took up positions on the Falls Road, it was announced that the army would end daytime patrolling in Belfast. The move was greeted as an important milestone in the peace process.

13 & 16 JANUARY & 15 MARCH 1995   THE INDEPENDENT

A quarter of a century of soldiering on

It was in August 1969 that Harold Wilson's Labour government gave the order, with the greatest reluctance, to send in troops to deal with the widespread disturbances raging in Belfast and in Londonderry's Bogside.

Wilson, as Prime Minister, agreed that if the then Northern Ireland Unionist government requested troops they would be dispatched. Jim Callaghan, the Home Secretary, was in mid-air in an RAF plane when the request came through.

Callaghan records in his memoirs that he was given a message scribbled on a signal pad: "It tersely informed us that an official request for the use of troops had been made. I immediately scribbled 'Permission granted' on the pad and handed it back to the navigator. A few minutes later General Freeland's troops began to relieve the police in the Bogside amid loud jubilation from the inhabitants."

In those days a pessimist was someone who thought the military intervention might last months rather than weeks. No one could have foreseen that it would endure for more than a quarter of a century. No one could have foreseen that the army would lose 500 lives, take 300 more, and develop into a permanent fixture for an entire generation.

The military establishment did not want to go in. Richard Crossman notes in his diaries that Denis Healey, the Defence Secretary, "was cagey and said on no account must we risk having to take over". Once in, the situation rapidly became worse rather than better.

In 1969 the army was supposed to be involved in a short-term peacekeeping mission. By 1972 Northern Ireland was almost out of control, with nearly 500 people dead in that year, nearly 100 of them soldiers. It was 1977 before something approaching stability was established and the death rate dropped appreciably.

The Troubles have been an inglorious job for the army as its principal enemy, the IRA, has frequently been perceived as holding the initiative. When the generals, or the privates, made errors they were often costly and made a bad situation worse, costing the lives of troops and civilians and increasing recruitment to the paramilitary groups.

Defenders of the army can argue that their presence may have prevented a much worse conflagration by containing the violence to manageable levels: this is in the realms of the unknowable. Over the years the troops got better training and equipment, but they never received much gratitude.

It became a cliché to say that the use of heavily armed soldiers was not the ideal way to deal with civil conflict within the United Kingdom, but no alternative ever emerged. The RUC was built up as a force large enough and well-protected enough to take on more and more responsibility, but there were always places such as west Belfast and south Armagh where police officers could not venture without military accompaniment.

More than 160 of the almost 500 military casualties of the Troubles have been killed in Belfast, more than half of these in the sprawling republican ghettos of the west of the city. Though troops will now be much less in evidence, those districts will remain studded with heavily protected military bases.

The move is the latest in a series of small but significant steps which are gradually transforming the city from a minor war zone into a more conventional metropolis. While the city still bears many scars and reminders of the 25 years of armed conflict which it has lived through, the many incremental relaxations of security have created a new atmosphere.

It would be inaccurate to say that normality has arrived, but since September 1994 only three people have died violently. The lack of violence has created new hope and removed much of the fear and apprehension which constantly attended life in Belfast.

The official approach has been to tread extremely carefully and to make no irreversible changes in security. But over the months the number of patrols has been gradually reduced, with soldiers largely discarding their helmets in favour of berets and a number of sealed-off streets reopened to traffic.

Searches and arrests also appear to be less common and the number of flights by helicopters is down, though they are still to be seen in the skies. Fewer of the army's very heavy vehicles are in evidence on the streets, while brightly coloured RUC cars and motorcycle patrolmen are to be seen in some districts previously considered too dangerous for non-armoured vehicles.

Security checkpoints are now something of a rarity. The decrease in terrorist activity means that more police officers are now available for traffic duties, which resulted in a rise in drink-driving detections over the Christmas period.

The move prompts the question of what the army is to do with the 11,700 troops whose active role is being drastically reduced. Soldiers will still be needed for night-time patrols and for guard duty at the many security installations and bases. They will also continue to be prominent in hardline republican areas such as south Armagh, where the RUC does not seem ready to take over completely.

The pace of the demilitarisation has been the object of much debate. Unionist representatives tend to favour as slow a response as possible, while Sinn Féin continually accuses the government of foot-dragging and delaying tactics. Constitutional nationalists call for a faster pace, arguing that speedier demilitarisation is the best way to consolidate the peace.

One problem is that, while peace has generally come to Northern Ireland, the political atmosphere remains highly charged. In such circumstances any moves involving troops are immediately seen as having heavy political overtones.

In the meantime, the troops released from patrolling and other duties appear likely to have much time on their hands. Some of the soldiers stationed in less troubled areas lead a reasonably comfortable existence, often living with their families in pleasant and generally safe surroundings.

But some of those in frontline areas, such as the Falls Road, are billeted in appalling conditions. North Howard Street base, a converted Victorian mill off the Falls Road, is dingy, cramped, noisy, overcrowded and suffering from cockroach infestation. When the *Independent* visited it in 1993, some soldiers said conditions were so bad that they actually preferred to be out on foot patrol to get away from them. They reported they routinely worked 16- or 18-hour days, while officers said the routine was basically one of work, eat and sleep.

The ending of daylight patrolling presumably means that many troops will now be shipped out of such barracks and into better conditions. And if the peace lasts, and political conditions allow it, it will probably not be long before some are on their way back to Britain.

POSTSCRIPT

The North Howard Street base was demolished in the autumn of 1995.

Although the violence had ceased, the troubles left a legacy of unresolved human rights issues. Most of these concerned alleged miscarriages of justice, but a major controversy arose around the case of Private Lee Clegg, a member of the Parachute Regiment.

The paratrooper was convicted of the murder of a teenage girl shot dead when he and other members of a patrol opened fire on a stolen car driven by a joyrider. When his conviction was upheld by the House of Lords, senior military figures and some British newspapers launched a major campaign for his release.

The case of Lee Clegg: middle England versus west Belfast

The case of Private Lee Clegg has once again shown up the yawning gulf in perceptions, values and fundamental sense of justice which exists between establishment Britain and nationalist Ireland.

Had the paratrooper been acquitted there would have been an outcry from nationalists. Instead, his conviction has produced an outcry from some of Britain's most senior military figures.

The Irish view is that someone has been held accountable for an incident in which two teenagers died: they should not have been travelling in a stolen car, but did not deserve the death penalty. Large sections of middle England, by contrast, view Private Clegg's life sentence as an extraordinary fate for a soldier doing a difficult job in dangerous circumstances.

One of the reasons for the gulf in perception is political: many people in Britain are inclined to support their army and disinclined to regard criticism of it as anything other than republican propaganda.

Much of middle England takes scant notice of media reports of soldiers doing something wrong. Many Irish nationalists, by contrast, subject the army's record to the most severe critical scrutiny, and habitually think the worst of it. Thus the clash of cultures: the man in Essex filters out the bad bits, while the man in west Belfast revels in sinister suspicions and conspiracy theories.

Many of the 300 people killed by the army over the 25 years of Troubles have been armed terrorists, about whom few tears are shed. But many others have been civilians, including children killed in a variety of controversial ways.

The authorities can point to the fact that there have been more than 30 prosecutions of members of the security forces involved in killings. The critics respond that Private Clegg is only the second soldier convicted of murder, and point out that the first, Private Ian Thain, was after a few years quietly released from prison and allowed to rejoin the army.

The critics cite this record as evidence that the legal system has been

64

deliberately designed to ensure the odds are deliberately stacked so as to make security force prosecutions rare and convictions even rarer. In other words, the charge is that after dubious incidents the authorities are more concerned with protecting army personnel than with achieving justice.

And though Essex man believes an injustice has been done by jailing the soldier, west Belfast man believes freeing him would be unjust. A nationalist councillor said: "People are quietly seething about the whole thing and they're convinced this guy is going to be let out. After all these years there's still disbelief that Britain can even think in these terms. It confirms the notion that the army is above the law, it confirms all the allegations that the authorities would never let British soldiers, whatever they had done, be brought to justice." Such indignation is all the greater since human rights lawyers, together with a government-appointed scrutinising committee, have for years been arguing that a lesser offence than murder should be available in such cases. The government has always turned down this idea.

Precedent has established that murder is the only charge that can be brought in such cases. Murder is the most serious charge in the law, and one of the most difficult to prove. Lord Colville QC, who has carried out a number of reviews of emergency legislation on behalf of the government, pointed out the dilemma several years ago: "The policeman or soldier, his family and friends, say that it is monstrous that a minor misjudgement in a man's reaction to a split-second emergency, should lead to a sentence of life imprisonment. But the victim's family and friends will be outraged by an acquittal."

The argument has been that the law should be changed so that troops involved in shooting incidents such as that in the Clegg case could, instead of murder, be charged with a spectrum of possible charges of varying gravity. Lord Colville, clearly sympathetic to the argument, noted: "If it led to the adoption of a lawful verdict between the extremes, the change would go some way to satisfying the community after such an incident, and would also be just to members of the security forces."

The army, however, strenuously resisted any such moves on the grounds that they would confuse soldiers and produce more court cases. A senior general, speaking privately several years ago, said: "In a whole lot of shootings the soldier is in great danger – danger of running foul of the law, danger to himself and his colleagues. Is it in the national interest to have soldiers more constrained? If he's to do his job properly it has to be simple, so I don't favour it. He's uniquely disadvantaged in the whole thing, so don't make his life any harder – if you do you'll have a weaker and less effective army." The present Clegg outcry is a direct result of the government's decision to accede to these arguments and not to introduce such laws.

The case is one of many in which the original army version of what happened

65

has been exposed as untruthful during subsequent court proceedings. In this case, in fact, it is almost certain that no prosecutions would have ensued had it not been for an RUC officer whose evidence the judge accepted as the only honest account of what took place. The general assumption in Britain is that Private Clegg and the other paratroopers opened fire because they believed they were under attack from the IRA. In fact they knew well enough that they faced not terrorists but joyriders, and never claimed at their trial that they believed the car contained IRA members.

The original trial involved six soldiers, including an officer. The judge in the no-jury proceedings heard that on 30 September 1990, Private Clegg was one of sixteen paratroopers accompanying the RUC officer on an anti-joyriding exercise in west Belfast. They were in an area plagued by joyriders, which one witness said "sounded like Brand's Hatch". The soldiers divided into teams, some setting up a checkpoint but discontinuing it after a stolen car drove through without stopping. As they were walking along a dark road another car appeared, and fire was opened on it.

The soldiers said they fired because they believed the lives of colleagues were in danger. All specifically testified that it had struck one of the defendants, Private Barry Aindow, on the leg. A large number of shots were fired, one of them killing the driver, 17-year-old Martin Peake, and two others fatally injuring a back-seat passenger, 18-year-old Karen Reilly.

The court heard that the RUC officer originally corroborated the soldiers' story, but later went to his superiors and made an 11-page statement in which he said that no one in the patrol was in any danger from the car, and that Private Aindow had not been struck by it. He also testified that the soldiers, apparently realising the circumstances of the shooting would get them into trouble, had deliberately caused an injury to Private Aindow's leg to fabricate evidence that he had been hit by the car. He said he heard a soldier being told, "Get down, you're it", and then saw another soldier stamp on his leg. A traveller who lived in a nearby caravan also gave evidence of seeing a soldier strike or appear to strike a colleague on the ground.

In his testimony, Private Clegg said he saw Private Aindow being knocked off balance, and had then fired four shots, three of them at the windscreen of the car as it was coming towards him, and one at the wing as it passed him. He denied firing at the rear of the car and denied firing the round which killed Miss Reilly, although the court heard forensic evidence that one of the shots which hit her came from his rifle and had passed through the rear of the vehicle.

He said that after firing the four shots he applied the safety catch and saw Private Aindow standing in a firing position, having also shot at the car. He could not explain how Private Aindow could have been knocked off balance, then taken aim and fired in such a short space of time.

Prosecuting counsel declared: "A soldier is in no different a position than that of any civilian, and where he discharges a firearm, where he intended to kill or seriously injure and death results, then he is guilty of murder unless it can be justified. Had it not been for the RUC constable on patrol with them and a civilian witness, and the forensic and pathological findings which triggered off the investigations, the means that these soldiers employed might have achieved their objective in covering their tracks."

The judge, in accepting the evidence of the RUC officer, said the shooting had not been premeditated and that Private Clegg had been presented with a situation not of his own making. He ruled that the first three shots had been legally fired, but that the fourth was fired at the back of the car at a time when it posed no threat.

Some reading this account will conclude that Private Clegg was guilty of murder; some that he was not guilty and should have been acquitted; some, perhaps, that some lesser offence than murder should be available, so that he would have received a lesser sentence.

The problem for ministers is that for a quarter of a century they have been arguing in Northern Ireland that murder is murder and that the law is the law, and that a cardinal principle of the British legal system is that soldiers are subject to the same laws as the public. The exercise of leniency and mercy for Private Clegg may now win the approval of middle England. As far as much of nationalist Ireland is concerned, however, such a course would be taken as final proof that there is one law for British soldiers and another for everyone else.

POSTSCRIPT

Clegg was given early release in July 1995, a decision which provoked extensive rioting in republican areas of Belfast.

At the same time as the Clegg issue, a rights issue of another kind came to the fore, centring on Queen's University Belfast, where many Protestants took

exception to moves designed to create a
more neutral atmosphere.

The controversy came as Northern
Ireland awaited a major political
development – publication of the
framework document in which the British
and Irish governments would lay out their
joint view of the future. The heat
generated by the university controversy
demonstrated the difficulties of satisfying
both sides.

The painful process of accommodation

It seems axiomatic that if the peace in Northern Ireland is to lead on to a new and lasting political settlement, the Unionist and nationalist communities will need to develop new respect for each other's traditions and sensitivities. One key problem in this lies in the deep-rooted belief, held by many, that any move made in response to nationalist requests almost automatically means a defeat for the Unionist cause.

A stark example of this has recently been filling the letter columns of Belfast newspapers. It centres on attempts to provide a more neutral atmosphere at Queen's University Belfast, which is both Northern Ireland's premier seat of learning and one of its biggest employers.

The issue has provided an important insight into the views of a politically almost silent section of society, the educated Protestant middle classes. It is illuminating in that it shows, in microcosmic form, what can happen when change is attempted.

68

The controversy surfaced in December 1994 when Queen's University announced that it was dropping the practice of having the band of the Royal Ulster Constabulary play the national anthem at its graduation ceremonies. The university said the anthem would still be played on other occasions, and that the RUC band would still perform at some of the ceremonies. It explained that the purpose of the move was "to promote a neutral working and social environment so that students, staff and visitors could feel comfortable".

The move followed years of complaints about the anthem from nationalist students, who were once in a minority but now make up around half the student body. A Catholic graduate explained: "They don't play the anthem in most English universities. We felt it was done to drive home who's boss, the fact that it didn't recognise that this significant other community, the nationalists, had views and rights."

A commentator in the moderate Unionist *Belfast Telegraph* confirmed the same point from a Protestant outlook: "The anthem has been regarded by the majority interest as a kind of musical totem, advising the other side in a suitably public and ceremonial manner that the land whereon they stand is British soil and that they would do well to remember it. It is part and parcel of the siege mentality. That mentality means that symbols of a disputed identity become inflated out of all proportion to their intrinsic significance."

The dropping of the anthem did not come out of the blue, but followed several very difficult years for Queen's. These began in 1989 when a report revealed that, although the percentage of Catholic students was growing, Catholics remained seriously underrepresented among its 3,000 staff.

More problems arrived as members of staff took a series of fair employment cases, alleging religious discrimination in appointments and promotions. Dealing with these cost Queen's hundreds of thousands of pounds: a couple of dozen more are still pending.

The university traditionally projected itself as above the sectarian and political fray, dismissing with disdain any suggestion of imbalance. But the evidence was too detailed to be ignored and, together with the accompanying financial cost and unwelcome publicity, forced a reluctant and painful reassessment.

Some in the Queen's hierarchy seemed unenthusiastic on the question of reform; others have changed their minds and have become determined to effect improvements. For example, in 1989 Professor Leslie Clarkson wrote to the *Independent* complaining of its coverage of the issue and declaring: "As an English-born academic I have been proud to work for 25 years in a university that has consistently striven to uphold the highest academic standards, often in very difficult circumstances. It saddens me that these efforts are undermined by insensitive journalism."

Now, as chairman of the university's new equal opportunities group, he admits discrimination was a problem. He is now widely recognised as a genuine advocate of change. Affirmative action programmes and other measures have already pushed up the number of locally recruited Catholics on the staff, so that many former critics now acknowledge that real efforts are being made.

Professor Clarkson now describes the background thus: "Historically, Queen's has been perceived as a Protestant university. It is still so perceived by many members of the Protestant community. Some people believe that Queen's should remain a bastion of Unionism, but the university is now endeavouring to ensure a truly harmonious working and social environment."

The dropping of the anthem is only one of a wide-ranging programme of changes, but it has stirred a storm of protest. Many came from Unionist politicians: Belfast City Council condemned the move; Ulster Unionist leader James Molyneaux turned down an honorary degree; the Rev Ian Paisley said it was outrageous and an insult; other politicians described it variously as sectarian, disgraceful, appalling, foolish, naïve, a concession to militant republicanism, and cultural triumphalism.

The Ulster Unionist Graduates Association said it should be seen as part of "an ongoing campaign to diminish the British ethos of Northern Ireland and to deprive the Ulster-British people of their heritage and culture. This is to be achieved through the pretence of a so-called neutral environment."

It was predictable that such reactions would come from political sources. What was more unusual was the tidal wave of letters from the normally silent middle classes: the *Belfast Telegraph* received more on this issue than on any other subject for a decade.

Anger, resentment and very often incomprehension about the move to drop the anthem leap from the scores of letters which have covered large expanses of newsprint. Former and present students and others, many of them silent throughout a quarter of a century of Troubles, have finally been moved to express a political opinion.

The anthem decision was the primary target, though exception was also taken to the move on the RUC band and the fact that the students' union has a number of bi-lingual signs in both English and Irish. There were many scathing criticisms of the fact that "God save the Queen" was to be replaced by Beethoven's "Ode to Joy", the European anthem.

"I graduated in 1955 and have been proud of my university until today," wrote a doctor now living in Lincoln. "We are British subjects; Queen's is a British university, established by Royal Charter 150 years ago. As British subjects, carrying out a duty authorised by our sovereign, we should acknowledge her position."

Another letter declared: "A surging tide of Irish republicanism is sweeping the university inexorably towards its final destination, a bastion of republicanism

70

where students of the Unionist tradition will be unwelcome." The students' union was "now a lost cause and an unwelcoming wilderness for anyone who believed in the United Kingdom. How long can it be before the Q is removed from QUB?"

Another correspondent wrote: "All students at Queen's know that Northern Ireland is still an integral part of the United Kingdom. If they don't like that why do they come to Queen's?" An elderly graduate announced he was sending back his degrees in protest and emotionally declared: "I would rather die than lose my national anthem."

Amid much criticism of the university authorities, others denounced the move as appeasement of republicans; as part of a co-ordinated campaign to "strip away part of the British identity"; complained that "Unionist sensibilities seem to count for nothing"; and claimed the students' union signs were designed to "culturally oppress and intimidate Unionists".

A few opposing voices were also heard. "I feel like a voice in the wilderness," wrote a mature student. "I think the decision courageous and correct." Another contended: "Those who fail to see that in neutral company the anthem is divisive are themselves part of the sectarian problem here, rather than part of the non-sectarian solution."

One letter writer asked with apparent passion: "Why don't we just go straight back to the 1960s and just start fighting all over again? Are these people for real? Is there something that slams down the shutters in the majority of Unionist minds as soon as there is the slightest move towards compromise? Is Unionist culture solely dependent on the subjugation of the minority?"

The Unionist community will soon be considering the framework document in which the British and Irish governments set out their joint vision of the future. Essentially, the deal on offer will be this: Northern Ireland will remain part of the UK so long as a majority want that; but within that framework the Unionist and nationalist traditions are both to be respected. It will set out, in other words, a mixed model where Unionists maintain their prized member-ship of the UK while nationalists have their Irishness formally expressed through continuing Dublin input, most visibly through new cross-border institutions.

The Queen's experience shows the difficulties involved in the metamorphosis of what was perceived as a Protestant-dominated institution into one in which all sections of the community might feel at home. The onset of peace has already helped improve the atmosphere in Belfast, but the anthem controversy shows how easy it is to touch deep-rooted and sensitive nerves, and how traumatic the coming years of negotiations will inevitably be. The task, in Northern Ireland as at Queen's, is to establish a new mixed culture in which concessions to one side are not necessarily seen as a defeat for the other.

The political temperature rose sharply in early February when, as the framework document was awaited, *The Times* published extracts from a draft of the document. The newspaper claimed it brought "the prospect of a united Ireland closer than it has been at any time since partition in 1920". This, naturally enough, alarmed Unionists.

John Major acted quickly, making a rare prime ministerial television broadcast to offer reassurance: "Judge our proposals as a whole. There is nothing you need fear."

This had little evident effect on Unionist politicians, most of whom declared in advance of seeing the document that they would not talk to the government on the basis of it. But despite what the Unionist MPs said, and despite the Queen's anthem controversy, other straws in the wind suggested that not everyone in the Protestant population favoured such a hard line.

Will peace melt Ulster's stiff soul?

The events of February – with all the alarums and excursions – may yet prove to be not just a time of high excitement but, conceivably, a moment of lasting significance. Time was when a revelation such as the leak to *The Times* would have been almost guaranteed to raise the Protestant temperature in Belfast to near boiling point, resulting in warlike noises and increased tension and violence.

Instead, the city was almost uncannily quiet. Its highly politicised citizens were certainly paying close attention to events at Westminster, but the furore created in London by Unionist MPs such as David Trimble and John Taylor was not matched by angry noises at home.

On this occasion, customarily aggressive dogs simply did not bark: and their silence may yet turn out to be the most significant feature of the whole affair. A Unionist community steeped in a culture of rejectionism decided, for once, to wait and see. Until now, Unionist politicians have often felt able to walk away from negotiations, secure in the knowledge that the electorate would not punish them for it. Most voters felt political talks had little chance of success and indeed little value. This afforded their politicians the luxury of feeling free, in most circumstances, to just say no.

Unionist representatives are already pledged to oppose plans for innovations such as cross-border bodies, on the grounds that such things would set them on the slippery slope to a united Ireland. Refusing to discuss the framework document with the government will not derail the peace process: both the IRA and loyalist ceasefires look fairly secure, and political activity will continue with or without the Unionists. But a blow will be struck against the idea of an inclusive peace process if the representatives of the larger part of the population opt out of participation.

That will come about if the Unionist community as a whole endorses the hard line of its MPs and concludes that the framework document represents a bridge too far. But will it? Unionist MPs are more known for their representational skills than qualities of leadership, and in the past have generally stayed in tune with their community. But this time there are real grounds for thinking, as the government hopes, that a gap exists between the MPs and their grassroots.

One loyalist militant summed up the mood in these terms: "There's a general opinion that the Unionists at Westminster have overreacted. In the main people want to see things being given a chance. They have grown used to peace. There are still a lot of anxieties, but people are happy with the peace." In other words, a powerful new element has entered the political scene. Old suspicions and anxieties have by no means disappeared, but now they exist alongside this tangible yearning to keep the peace alive. Unionist politicians may now be called upon to be something more than mere tribal champions.

The contrast with the political scene of just a few months ago is remarkable. Just last October James Molyneaux was fêted by his party at its annual conference in Carrickfergus, Co Antrim. In one of the most embarrassing moments of this shy politician's career, overexuberant Young Unionists took to the floor and, to the strains of Tina Turner's "Simply the Best", danced and waved photographs of him in the air.

The moment, though well-meant, was clearly something of a personal nightmare for a politician who is one of the most low-key and self-effacing in these islands. Actively proud of his low profile, he once told a journalist: "I'm the dull dog of Ulster politics and nobody takes much notice of what I say." He later telephoned the reporter to make sure he included the remark in his story.

This was intended to convey that while he had neither the vocal capability nor the desire to compete with the Rev Ian Paisley in a decibel contest, he achieved much more in his own quiet way. In other words, he preferred to work discreetly in the corridors of power to which he gained access by virtue of the nine valuable Commons votes he commanded. His projection was that this gave him great influence with John Major, and that the Unionist cause was thus being unobtrusively but inexorably advanced.

Recent events – the impact of the leak on the Anglo-Irish framework document, and the intense fever of activity which followed – at first seemed to be in his party's favour, if not in his own. The first reaction was that the Ulster Unionists had received a timely warning that their interests were not being protected by the Molyneaux–Major relationship, and been given an opportunity to turn the tables. As the week ended, however, the signs were that it had in fact been a disastrous week for the cause of traditional Unionism.

The leak is presumed to have come from someone high in government who regarded the framework document as anti-Unionist and who hoped to sabotage it. The effect was the opposite. It resulted in almost complete isolation of the Unionists in the Commons, where they effectively coalesced the entire spirit of Westminster against them. John Major's subsequent television broadcast was widely interpreted in Britain as a gallant bid to save the peace process, though in fact neither of the ceasefires looks to be in the slightest danger. His action further firmly identified the type of north–south structures envisaged in the document with the wider cause of peace.

A series of aggressive television appearances by Mr Taylor and Mr Trimble were completely counterproductive for British audiences, eliciting not sympathy but irritation at what was perceived as their unyielding negativity. One London-based Unionist said despairingly: "They lost us support and sympathy every time they opened their mouths."

Mr Molyneaux's response was less angry and couched in his characteristic ambivalent style, leading one observer to remark: "As usual, Jim burnt no boats." In this he seems, whether by accident or design, to reflect the more open-minded mood back in Belfast. The faint praise which some of his MPs offered Mr Molyneaux, and the characterisation that he had been shamefully treated by Mr Major was seen by many as laying the ground for more open criticism of his leadership. Even as the Young Unionists were prancing in front of Mr Molyneaux last October, one party critic privately growled: "We're not getting enough from the deal. Molyneaux's long view is too long, too slow. The next two years is the time to capitalise on our influence."

Mr Molyneaux may now stand accused of having placed too much trust in a wily and untrustworthy Mr Major, and not having pushed him enough. Traditionally most Unionist leaders have fallen because they have been too soft and not militant enough: Mr Taylor and Mr Trimble thus seem well placed to take advantage of such a situation.

Yet although the IRA cessation of violence happened less than six months ago, the atmosphere has already been greatly changed. The original caution which greeted the ceasefire developed into relief and then – with classic northern Irish inhibition – a sort of suppressed near-euphoria. There has still been no dancing in the streets and no exuberant displays of celebration. There is still anxiety that something could go wrong, and still less than complete confidence that the violence has gone for good.

But there is also, in many quarters, a deep appreciation of the benefits of peace and the desire to maintain it is palpable and fervent. The prevailing belief is that the ceasefires are for real and that an unprecedented opportunity now exists for a new start.

In the past Unionists have often opposed British initiatives, sometimes successfully. In 1974, when the Heath government introduced new arrangements along similar lines to the framework document's ideas, a Protestant general strike brought the country to a standstill and led to its abandonment. Protestant objections to the 1985 Anglo-Irish agreement were just as intense but the loyalist campaign against it, though protracted, was disorganised and ultimately unsuccessful. Nonetheless, the thought has continued to lurk in the Unionist psyche that the force of Protestant numbers can, if properly mobilised, thwart the wishes of British governments.

This time round, however, there are grounds for believing that Protestant reactions may be more thoughtful and considered. The major Unionist parties have already committed themselves to outright rejection, but the once-violent loyalist paramilitary groups are now displaying a much more open mind. In place of the standard dire threats, they are now appealing for calm.

Much of the Unionist business community is surprisingly pragmatic about innovative north–south links, and even prepared to consider whether they might offer desirable new openings for trade. And above all is that new constraint: the sense that nothing should be done to jeopardise the peace. One Protestant clergyman said: "They're hoping against hope that it will hold. People are just quietly waiting. They're holding their breath and there's quite an edgy mood: a lot depends on how the politicians play it."

His comments reflected the importance of presentation and micro-management of just how something as vital as the framework document is presented to a community which is so nervous of innovation and so prone to volatile mood swings. A couple of ill-considered ministerial comments could spell disaster.

Six months ago the IRA faced its moment of truth, gauging whether to continue with terrorism or to pursue its aims by peaceful means. Gerry Adams and the other republican leaders opted for politics and in the short time since then have already built many new political relationships. The framework document looks like becoming the basis of a consensus on how to proceed, and will form the common factor of the approaches of the two governments, the Clinton administration, Irish-America and the European Union.

People in the Unionist community say privately, in a way their MPs do not say publicly, that they worry that a purely negative reaction to the document would mean consigning themselves to a new phase of isolation which would be both uncomfortable and unproductive, and which would cast a shadow on the prospects for lasting peace.

Going down that road would lead to confrontation with the government and all those other forces, and would lead to Unionism being accused, fairly or unfairly, as being against peace. The Unionist MPs have yet to explain how their community would gain from such an approach: they might help to bring down the government, but there is little prospect that the next British government would be any more disposed to their view.

Most immediately, the two governments are now pushing ahead fast to complete the document which will provide a critical test of whether the enthusiasm for peace will herald a new willingness to consider compromise. In deciding to make his television broadcast, John Major clearly calculated that daylight had opened up between Unionist leaders and their electorate. Over the years a number of Prime Ministers and Northern Ireland Secretaries have toyed with this notion, and wondered whether they could exploit a gap between politicians and voters. In almost all instances they were wrong: no such gaps existed, or if they did they snapped shut when election time came around and traditional voting patterns reasserted themselves. This time it could be different: this time the grassroots may tell their MPs that the time has come to work towards a new political settlement to protect the prize of peace.

In February John Major and John Bruton came to Balmoral in south Belfast to launch the framework document. In 1912 a previous Tory leader, Bonar Law, had stood on the same site to express solidarity with Unionism in what one historian described as "no less than the wedding of Protestant Ulster with the Conservative and Unionist party". The angry Unionist reaction to the document was, however, evidence enough that a divorce had since taken place.

It was a key publication, representing as it did the considered opinion of the two governments on the way ahead.

At the crossroads of Irish history

John Major and John Bruton launch their governments' joint vision of the way ahead

One thing above all else sets the framework document apart from all others in the litany of unsuccessful initiatives which stud the history of the Troubles: it was launched in a time of peace. All the others were unveiled against a background of bombs and bullets, the audible signs of conflict and division. The republican terrorists and loyalist paramilitants are still out there, but their guns are silent.

There is no guarantee that it will work, and it could be months before it is clear whether it has or has not. But if it does the guns could be silenced for ever, bringing the blessed prize of peace to Ireland. The bulk of the population regards the absence of violence as something to be treasured and fervently hopes it will continue. The hope of the two governments is that this will translate into a new readiness to take risks and contemplate compromises.

As with past initiatives, it will have to survive days of initial battering and suspicion-laden scrutiny. Even before publication Unionist politicians had, in time-honoured Belfast fashion, got their retaliation in first and condemned it. The government's hope is that the Protestant grassroots will take a more measured view and move away from the politics of instant denunciation.

The communal desire for peace is so palpable that there are grounds for thinking this is not a forlorn hope, and that Unionist voters may be more open-minded than their politicians. But this will be a tense time, with uncertainty co-existing with hope: the power of peace to change hearts and minds is about to be tested.

Complete rejection by the Protestant community would be a severe setback, for apart from the Rev Ian Paisley almost all the major political elements have until now, at least notionally, been part of the process. A flat Protestant "no" would not end the process and would not immediately threaten the ceasefires, but it would create a precarious imbalance.

It would also cast Unionist leaders in confrontation with yet another British government. Edward Carson, one of Unionism's historical heroes, once forecast that its last battle would be against the forces of the crown. The present situation is unlikely to develop that far, but Unionists have a clear folk memory of thwarting British governments in past tests of will. Their politicians were yesterday beginning the task of doing so again.

The Troubles are littered with British initiatives, many of them undertaken with much reluctance. In 1969 British troops had to be sent in to reimpose order in the wake of large-scale communal strife. In 1972, after much hesitation, Edward Heath decided to make a fresh start and abolished the Unionist-dominated Stormont parliament.

Mr Heath's purpose was to dismantle the one-party system under which Unionists ruled a resentful Catholic and nationalist minority. As an alternative he and William Whitelaw, the first Northern Ireland Secretary, developed a new system with, fascinatingly, the same three central elements as have reappeared in the framework document.

The document differs in detail from the Sunningdale agreement of 1973–4, but it is clearly in direct line of descent from it. Sunningdale was hammered out by the two governments and three of the main Northern Ireland parties. It was fiercely attacked by Mr Paisley and most Unionist politicians on the one hand, and by the IRA on the other.

The first of its three main elements dealt with the terms of the union, in effect setting out that Northern Ireland would remain part of the United Kingdom for the foreseeable future. This took the form of declarations that Northern

Ireland would stay part of the UK while a majority of its people desired it. If a majority voted against this at some future stage, it would become part of a united Ireland.

The second element was that a new Belfast administration would include both Unionists and nationalists. One section of Unionism, led by the late Brian Faulkner, agreed to form a powersharing executive together with the SDLP and the middle-of-the-road Alliance party.

Thirdly, north–south relations were to be put on an institutionalised footing through a new "Irish dimension". A Council of Ireland with seven northern and seven southern ministers was to be established, with powers which were expected to grow as time passed. A new 60-strong cross-border consultative assembly was to be appended to the council.

The underlying theory was that Unionists would value the assurance on the union. Nationalists were not to have a united Ireland, but would have the substantial consolations of participation in government and formal recognition of their Irish identity through the council.

It all fell apart in less than six months. Most of the Protestant population were not reassured on the union and deeply disliked the constitutional novelties of powersharing and the Irish dimension. A widely supported loyalist general strike run by loyalist politicians, paramilitary groups and trade unionists brought down the executive before the Council of Ireland could be established.

The sudden collapse of these carefully crafted structures caused many to conclude glumly that Northern Ireland was a problem without a solution. Over the following decade government initiatives tended to be half-hearted affairs, generally fizzling out at the exploratory stage as ministers concluded there was little possibility of agreement.

The exception was the 1985 Anglo-Irish agreement which, in the teeth of Unionist disapproval and resistance, established a strong Irish dimension. This was in direct line of descent from Sunningdale: the guarantee on the union was repeated, together with an offer that agreement on a new powersharing executive would reduce the Irish government's role. The offer was not taken up.

In the framework document the three familiar pillars – maintenance of the union, participatory government and north–south links – once again re-emerged into view. The promise of continuing union is still there; the word powersharing has been avoided but the concept remains; and the Council of Ireland is now called a "north–south body".

The similarity of language is striking. The Sunningdale agreement spoke of "a Council of Ireland with executive and harmonising functions and a consultative role". The framework document says the north–south body will "discharge or oversee delegated executive, harmonising or consultative functions". Both envisage an entity which would grow in stature as time went on.

80

Clearly, two decades of Unionist opposition have not changed the view of both London and Dublin that these remain the key elements of a settlement.

Nor have two decades of republican violence altered these tenets. The recent focus on Unionist reactions to the document has diverted attention from the fact that most of the new hope in Belfast has flowed from the IRA ceasefire. Without that the bombs would still be going off, and much of the population would have cynically dismissed the launch as just another doomed enterprise, not worth raising hopes or taking risks for. Now, for all the uncertainty and anxieties, the chances of progress have been appreciably strengthened.

In 1973 the IRA rejected the Sunningdale agreement and pledged that the "armed struggle" would continue, as indeed it did for a further two decades. Yesterday, faced with a Sunningdale-style package, Gerry Adams did not urge his people back to the barricades but instead promised to study it carefully.

The framework document is not at all what republicans ideally wanted to see. What they wanted to hear from John Major was a solemn declaration that Britain was on the way out of Ireland: but they knew that was never on the cards. They have come a long way from the days when they routinely dismissed anything short of withdrawal as merely tinkering with the problem. Mr Adams has led his people from a futile pursuit of military victory to the sober reality that the way ahead lies in making a start on building relationships with those they previously fought.

In the republican community it was Mr Adams who took the initiative and, in a terribly slow way, gradually persuaded his people to lay the guns aside. He and others regularly complain that Unionism has produced no De Klerk to lead the Protestant community towards a new accommodation: certainly no such figure is emerging.

Unionists face a crucial choice. They instinctively recoil from all-Ireland institutions, fearing that they inexorably lead towards Irish unity; and they traditionally doubt British assurances that this is not the case. But it is also obvious to them that the peace process, with its widespread support, has a momentum which may be slowed but is unlikely to be halted. Their fear is that, if they opt out, they will be heading for futile isolation and allowing their own future to be mapped out without them.

The unpalatable conclusion of Unionists reading the document is almost bound to be that the union with Britain, as they have traditionally known it, is no longer on offer to them. John Major, a prime minister who calls himself a Unionist, has after the most detailed consideration brought forward a document with an unmistakable all-Ireland orientation.

He has made it plain that they can stay in the UK so long as they wish; but while they do, they should appreciate that life can be expected to take on a steadily greener hue. The clear signal has also been sent that while Britain will not cast them out, nor will it be beseeching them to stay.

If Unionism does opt for a new departure, and this time accepts what it rebuffed at the time of Sunningdale, the impetus will have to come from the grassroots and not from the top down. The government's hope lies in the new ingredient of peace, and in the premise that the Protestant community has learnt more than have its political representatives from the last quarter-century of conflict. Six months ago republicanism made its choice, opted for a historic compromise and decided on an end to violence. It is now Unionism's turn to stand at the crossroads.

The framework document dismayed Unionist politicians and probably made inevitable the later departure of James Molyneaux as leader of the Ulster Unionist party. Mr Molyneaux had assumed that Mr Major had been persuaded to take a Unionist line: in this he was shown to be very wrong.

25 FEBRUARY 1995   THE INDEPENDENT

The week John Major went nationalist

This was the week, a historic one for Anglo-Irish relations, when John Major pulled the plug on the leaders of Unionism, some of whom fondly regarded him as an ally, and aligned himself with modern Irish nationalist theory.

Despite his repeated assertions that he is himself a Unionist, the framework document he unveiled was a comprehensive and undisguised rejection of all the principal Unionist political theories. It blasted them out of the water by opting for an all-Ireland approach.

British governments have produced many documents designed to balance the demands of Unionist and nationalist politicians, but this was not one of them. Although the surrounding rhetoric is mostly aimed at soothing Unionists, the actual text of the document contained no attempt at symmetry. Northern Ireland is not to have joint authority, if by that is meant 50–50 rule by London and Dublin, and it is to remain in the union. But the terms of that union are to be changed to introduce a new dispensation with a whole new philosophy and system of government.

In deciding on this course Mr Major's behaviour has followed a similar path to that of Margaret Thatcher, who began by asserting that "Northern Ireland is as British as Finchley" and wound up being burnt in effigy by loyalists for signing the Anglo-Irish agreement.

So why did Mr Major, who should be anxious to have the nine Ulster Unionist MPs supporting him in the Commons lobbies, come to reject so decisively the policies of Unionist leader James Molyneaux? The answer lies in the fact that Unionism's arguments and vision of the future were carefully considered, and found wanting.

The basic proposition of the two governments is that a lasting settlement will not come about without an inclusive new system of government to which everyone, or almost everyone, can give their allegiance. The Rev Ian Paisley, with his appetite for discord and division, has clearly never been in the business of helping construct such a system. Between Mr Paisley and Mr Molyneaux there are substantial differences of style and content, not to mention volume, but also many points of similarity.

The bottom line is that neither has any sign of an equality agenda and neither shows any sign of producing an offer which stands a chance of meeting the concerns of even moderate nationalists. Neither is thinking of working towards an agreed political settlement. Neither is going to do a deal capable of making nationalists feel at home in Northern Ireland: there is simply no give there.

In the past these basic facts were obscured by the IRA's campaign of terrorism, but since the ceasefires the question of a willingness to compromise has assumed central importance. Out there in the general Protestant community things are stirring and some attitudes are being re-examined, but this has not been reflected by the Unionist MPs.

The opposite has been the case. All along they predicted the peace process would come to nothing, with Mr Molyneaux a year ago describing it as "a dead Christmas tree". Far from welcoming the cessations, they clearly regarded them as problematic and unsettling, leading many to suspect they almost preferred the old certainties of conflict. One of the MPs complained recently: "We've been outflanked by peace." In short, the approach of the Unionist politicians bears no promise of leading towards an inclusive settlement. Balanced against this, on the other hand, has been a persuasive set of arguments coming from nationalists.

For more than two decades nationalist theoreticians such as Garret FitzGerald and John Hume have been accepting that Irish unity could only ever come about with the consent of a majority in Northern Ireland. (Consent was the buzzword of the week: it occurs in the framework document at least 10 times.) This approach shifted the focus away from the idea of pursuing the territorial unity of Ireland towards that of reconciling its differing traditions.

This theory superseded the traditional nationalist belief that the British presence was the root cause of the problem, and thus made it easier for Dublin and London to co-operate. The continuing violence had the effect of bringing the British and Irish establishments closer together, the 1985 Anglo-Irish agreement demonstrating their growing sense of partnership. The two governments came to regard Northern Ireland as a problem which was best jointly managed.

Another strong factor was that, viewed from London, the south was becoming a steadily less threatening place. The power of the Catholic church has been draining away for years, while the intelligentsia has placed more and more store on the rights of Unionists. Dublin is a cosmopolitan European city where European unity is spoken of far more often than Irish unity: the Republic is fast modernising itself.

All this made Britain more responsive to the argument that, in return for the ever more open acknowledgement of the consent principle, formal recognition was needed of the Irish aspiration of those 39 per cent of Northern Ireland voters who support nationalist parties.

This was true even as the violence raged, and indeed those who drew up the framework document say it was scarcely changed at all after last year's cessations. But the ending of violence has transformed the atmosphere and created almost universal pressure for compromise and new beginnings: the changed circumstances mean it is not just purely theoretical but also a means of consolidating the peace.

The immobilism of the Unionist MPs led to their isolation in the Commons, as they refused to join the consensus that a truly historic opportunity for peace exists if, as seems entirely possible, the nationalist community coalesces around the notion of change by peaceful means only.

The reaction of the general Protestant community has not been so unremittingly negative. The old cry of sellout is still to be heard in the land, but so too are other Protestant voices saying that the tide is moving, that the time has come to negotiate the best deal they can; that in the cause of peace they can

84

live with something along the lines of the framework document. Such sentiments may be the first small signs that John Major is correct in believing that not all Unionists are as hardline as their political leaders.

In contrast to Unionist politicians, republicans seemed reasonably pleased with the framework document. Their *ard-fheis* (annual conference) showed how far they had come in a short space of time.

---

27 FEBRUARY 1995   THE INDEPENDENT

Ballot box makes ground on the Armalite

This was the first Sinn Féin *ard-fheis* which, for the leadership at least, was just about politics. It wasn't about big cheers for the IRA; it didn't feature Gerry Adams solemnly warning that the armed struggle would go on for as long as Britain remained in Ireland.

On the same spot as Danny Morrison once exhorted his party to think of taking power in Ireland with an Armalite rifle in one hand and a ballot paper in the other, Mr Adams declared: "The IRA's initiative was a brave one. To sue for peace is a noble thing." The violence went on for so long that the republicans, like everyone else, could scarcely remember life without it. To begin with, Sinn Féin was little more than a legal flag of convenience for the IRA, but during the 1980s the party developed into a substantial adjunct to the IRA until, at some stage, the tail started wagging the dog.

In 1994 the republican leadership decided, for a variety of reasons, that a feasible alternative existed to the armed conflict and, in the words of Mr Adams, sued for peace. This *ard-fheis* represented an important step in the movement

Martin McGuinness of Sinn Féin talks to the grassroots at his party's *ard-fheis*

of Sinn Féin away from making up one half of a political–paramilitary double act towards more conventional politics. That shift still has a fair way to go but the republican leadership, headed by Mr Adams and Martin McGuinness, shows no sign whatever of retreating from the decision to go political.

But this is very much a transitional phase, and the message from some in the hall was that not everyone in the movement is so completely convinced that politics alone is the way ahead. The attendance was the best for years and there were the usual standing ovations for Mr Adams and Mr McGuinness but there was also, for the first time since the ceasefire, public criticism of the peace process from within the movement.

Sinn Féin conferences are even more shamelessly stage-managed than those of the Conservative party and the main debate opened with no fewer than six consecutive speeches from leadership figures. By the time they were through the chairman was saying sorrowfully that, due to time pressures, other speakers could, alas, have only a minute and a half each.

This was, however, time enough for the dissident voices to be heard. Three Dublin delegates, one of whom works for Sinn Féin's own weekly paper, *Republican News*, stood up in turn and said there was suspicion and concern about the peace process. One argued that the British government had not shifted on fundamentals and that the process would not lead to the British withdrawal they wanted. Another said the danger was that republicans would find themselves involved in a lengthy process which in the end would fall far short of their goal. A third said the strategy was damaging the "freedom struggle" and was a short cut which could not work.

The republicans have always prided themselves that they, principally through the IRA, have in their language provided a dynamic for movement. The leadership is now in the business of arguing that Sinn Féin is alone capable of doing this, as a major player now firmly at the centre of the political action. The assertion is that this political action will inexorably lead towards eventual British disengagement.

The amount of applause for the dissidents seemed to suggest, however, the existence of a widespread fear that the process would not go so far. "The British government still reaffirms the Unionist veto," said one. "Imagining or inventing conditions which don't exist is not a way forward," said another.

These are people who come from a culture accustomed to thinking in terms of eventual victory. At no stage did Mr Adams confidently promise them such victory: rather, he spoke of a search for agreement and a process of negotiations with no predetermined outcome.

He and the leadership have made their choice for the future, but not everyone in the ranks seems ready to regard the violence as a chapter definitively closed. He and the IRA have declared for peace, but it seems that part at least of this profoundly militaristic movement still hankers after the old certainties of the gun and bomb, and has misgivings about embarking with Mr Adams in his long march towards conventional politics.

Spring brought a poignant reminder that although the violence had come to an end, the suffering of many people had not.

The scars
that may never heal

Mrs May Seymour at her husband Jim's funeral on 4 March 1995

For 22 years Jim Seymour lay in a Tyrone hospital bed, a bullet in his head, apparently conscious but unable to move or speak; and every day for 22 years his wife May visited him. According to a relative: "Sometimes he would smile and sometimes he would cry and that was all the response she ever got from him."

Jim Seymour died last week at the age of 55, bringing the 22-year vigil to a close: the strain and anguish suffered by him and his family can only be imagined. As with so many families, the scars inflicted may never heal.

In 1973 Mr Seymour was an RUC constable, on guard duty at Coalisland RUC station a few miles from his home at Ballynakelly, Co Tyrone, when it was attacked by the IRA. A bullet came through an observation slit and hit him between the eye and the ear, lodging in his skull.

In a newspaper interview eight years ago Mrs Seymour described first seeing him after the shooting: "I'd never have known him. His head was swollen to twice the size. He was black to the waist with congealed blood. I could hardly see him for machines, all the machines of the day connected to him. I can't get that picture out of my mind. My heart is broken but I try not to think of them that shot my husband. What do they care about grief?"

Mr Seymour was a Devon man who served for 12 years in the Royal Navy before moving to Northern Ireland. From early on after the shooting it was clear he would spend the rest of his life in hospital. Relatives said they were unable to tell whether he ever really knew what had happened to him. His sister-in-law, Mrs Edith Simpson, said: "There was never any hope of Jim making a recovery. He could hear and he knew what was going on around him. He enjoyed television, but because of his condition he simply couldn't communicate."

In the early days Mrs Seymour, having no car, walked two miles every day to catch a bus to the hospital. Afterwards she walked the two miles back home again. Later she learnt to drive and made the journey by car, year after year, as generations of doctors and nurses cared for her husband during his two decades in South Tyrone Hospital.

During that time his children, who were aged 12 and eight when he was shot, grew up, married, and had children of their own. After their weddings they drove to the hospital to have photographs taken with him. Ernie Simpson, Mr Seymour's brother-in-law, told a local paper: "When the children had their wedding photographs taken with Jim it was desperate to watch. He just managed a wee smile."

Mrs Seymour visited every day. According to Mr Simpson: "Her love for Jim only seemed to grow stronger when he became ill. You just could not put into words the affection she had for that man. It was her life's duty. In the same way other people get up in the morning to go to work, she got up to visit Jim. She looked forward to it. She'd hold his hand and talk away to him about family problems, marriages, deaths, all the news."

Mrs Simpson added: "She told him about the ceasefires, but we'll never know if he understood or not. There is great sadness, and I suppose it's even more heartbreaking now that there is peace in the country." The end, when it came, contained a final cruel blow. Mrs Seymour had visited her husband as usual that day and returned home, not realising he was close to death. The news that he had died came unexpectedly and devastated her.

Although the Seymour family has suffered particularly severely from the Troubles, their protracted heart-rending tragedy is only one of hundreds arising from a quarter-century of death and destruction.

Among the wounded are many in wheelchairs or confined to bed, or who have suffered brain damage. Some are in constant pain. One senior policeman continued to serve in the force despite losing an arm, a leg and an eye in an explosion. Another officer has no arms. One IRA volunteer was emasculated in a premature blast.

The horror a bomb can cause was summed up in this report of an explosion at the Abercorn restaurant in Belfast in the 1970s: "One girl has lost both legs, an arm and an eye. Her sister has lost both legs. A male victim lost two legs, and a female lost one leg and one arm. Another female lost one limb and three of the injured have lost eyes."

Most of the killings were the work of terrorists, but one of the deepest sources of resentment and sense of injustice is to be found among some of the several hundred families which lost members at the hands of the security forces. The perception that soldiers carried out unjustified killings, and escaped prosecution for them, has been one of the wellsprings of the Troubles.

So many people have been treated unkindly by fate. At least two women have lost two life partners, both killed by terrorists years apart. One woman survived a shooting but lost her unborn child which was buried, in a tiny light blue coffin, in unconsecrated ground next to a graveyard only yards from her home.

Over and over again the "wrong" people died. A nine-year-old Londonderry boy, playing cowboys with his brother, upset a tripwire in his garden and set off a bomb which killed him. A man burst into a house in Belfast, shot dead the occupant, then exclaimed, "Christ, I'm in the wrong house." A man was issued with a personal protection weapon after receiving threats from loyalists: within a few hours it went off by accident and killed him. A dying man said to his wife: "The bastards, why did they shoot me? I'm not in anything." A bullet fired by a soldier during a fight in a pub passed through the arm of a loyalist activist and killed a man having a quiet drink in a corner. A bullet fired by a republican passed through the arm of a policeman on traffic duty and killed an Asian woman motorist.

The senselessness of many of the killings is increased by the character of some of the killers. A loyalist, jailed for four murders, had been drinking two bottles of gin a day which resulted in brain damage. He gave himself up to police after twice trying to commit suicide.

90

One woman lost her son, shot dead by loyalists, and her husband, who collapsed and died when he heard the news. When a father of four was shot dead in Co Armagh his widow and her sister had to be carried into church for the funeral, for both women suffered from multiple sclerosis. A drunk man followed his wife to a police station, became involved in an altercation with a sentry, and was shot dead.

There are hundreds more stories of terrible deaths and terrible injuries, of shattered lives and shattered families, of widows and orphans whose suffering continues though the guns have fallen silent. The hope must be that, whatever lies ahead, their experiences should serve as a lasting reminder of why Northern Ireland should not return to violent conflict, a lasting reminder of the sadness and the pity of it all, a lasting reminder that war is hell.

Six months on, the IRA ceasefire was holding, though opinions differed on how secure the peace was.

17 MARCH 1995   THE INDEPENDENT

Widespread hope
may spike guns for good

Sir Patrick Mayhew, the Northern Ireland Secretary, has been giving dire warnings about the IRA. He recently told Americans: "It is still in being, still maintains its arsenal, is still recruiting, targeting and training, still seeking funds."

There is little reason to doubt that this is so. The IRA, one of the world's most dangerous and long-lived terrorist organisations, is still out there with a fearsome capacity to kill and destroy. So too are the loyalist groups who carried out so many assassinations.

Furthermore, neither set of terrorists has been given any guarantees that the peace process will eventually lead to what they want, a united Ireland or firmer links with Britain. The fact that these goals are so obviously mutually exclusive illustrates the magnitude of the problems ahead.

Given these bare facts, an outside observer could be forgiven for surmising that the peace process balances precariously on a knife edge. The population, one might think, must be in constant fear and trembling that at any minute the guns will open up again. Yet that perception is a million miles from the actual impression registered by both the resident population and visitors. On the streets of Belfast and elsewhere, the prevailing assumption is simply that it's probably over for good.

There are many reasons why people have, by various paths, come to hold that viewpoint. Some simply hope and pray that the violence won't return. Some watch Gerry Adams's triumphal progress when he visits America and realise that a return to violence would sweep away his credibility and the new alliances he has forged.

Some believe that all the appalling bloodshed, with its inconclusive outcome, has driven home the lesson, the hard way, that there could be no real winners. Others simply react to the atmosphere, revelling in the fact that so many of the old tensions have been gradually draining away. Some remember the near-universal relief that greeted the ceasefires, and bank on that. There has been no single moment of celebration. The IRA cessation of last August was an electric moment, but it was characterised by hope rather than euphoria. At the time it left many unanswered questions: Will it hold? Why have they stopped? Do they mean it?

The loyalist ceasefire of October was another milestone. When Gusty Spence, a one-time loyalist assassin from the 1960s, offered "the loved ones of all innocent victims over the past 25 years abject and true remorse", a new note was struck, a new tone was set.

Even the double ceasefire was not enough to start the celebrations. Once again there were so many questions in the air, centring on whether the hard men on both sides really could accept, after a quarter of a century of bloodshed, that it was all over. But as each death-free month has passed, confidence has grown that the peace will last.

The striking thing is how the sense that peace is here to stay has grown in spite of the indisputable facts outlined by Sir Patrick. The terrorists have not gone away, yet there is an increasing acceptance that what is crucial is not the terrorist armouries, but the will to use them.

At the moment much of the political focus is on IRA weaponry. But on the streets the view is widespread – though by no means universal – that neither the IRA nor the loyalists have any plans to draw the guns from the dumps and

92

go back to the war. In other words, a communal view is emerging that, guns or no guns, this is a meaningful peace process. The realisation is also dawning that the arms issue is only one of a series of formidable issues to be dealt with along the long road to a political settlement.

In the framework document the British and Irish governments sent a strong joint signal outlining the type of mixed model of administration which they envisage for Northern Ireland, and for Anglo-Irish relations. The Unionist parties rejected this but are nonetheless prepared to discuss their own proposals. Round-table talks are not in the offing, but the next 12 months are expected to see a whole series of bilateral meetings. Unless something happens to galvanise the whole scene – which is not impossible – round-table encounters are unlikely this side of the next British general election.

But talking is the order of the day: a culture of jaw-jaw is replacing war-war. Belfast is already, in fact, suffering from conference blight as the Northern Ireland chattering classes flit from session to seminar, from plenary to workshop. The conferences, which are held most weekends, range over the post-Troubles issues of demilitarisation, future policing, human rights, of rebuilding the economy, of new political structures.

The people on the street may not have the same detailed interest in constitution-building, but the same sense is there that something has changed, probably irrevocably. The changes have brought peace, but they have not brought political consensus. Republicans are still republicans; loyalists are still loyalists. Their aims are still far apart, and finding an accommodation will depend on building on the peace to achieve political agreement. The politicians never managed to agree in the past, on many occasions simply walking away from the table without incurring penalties from their voters.

This time it could be different: if the communal support for peace lasts and grows, there will be community pressure to stick to the task of finding the long-elusive accommodation. Already the overwhelming message is clear: that there should be no return to the bad old days. The next step, which will not be easy, will be finding the political compromises necessary to secure the peace.

May saw the appearance of a book by Gerry Adams. Published by Brandon Press, *Free Ireland: Towards a Lasting Peace* gave an insight into the evolution of the republican leader.

From dogmatic youth to flexible innovator

B ack in 1969, Gerry Adams muses in this book, he was "maybe too young and too dogmatic". He portrays himself, back in those days, as trying out various non-violent political methods – marches, protests, housing agitation, squatting.

As early as page 28, however, comes the chapter with the unoriginal title of "From reform to revolution", and from then on the IRA and Sinn Féin take centre stage. Mr Adams's career was anything but dogmatic and unoriginal as he proved himself the most flexible and innovative republican leader of the century.

His leadership skills helped first to maintain the republican movement as a fearsome and deadly fighting machine, and more recently helped persuade his movement that it was time for the killing to stop. It is possible to commend him for the second achievement while condemning him for the first.

Free Ireland is for the most part written in an easy, open style which is in welcome contrast to the opaqueness of many of the deliberately indistinct speeches he delivered in the run-up to the IRA ceasefire. The book is a reissue of a 1986 work in which he laid out what was then standard republican theory. Two chapters bring it up to date.

Without armed struggle, he wrote in 1986, the issue of Ireland would not even be an issue. In those days the metaphor was of the hammer and the anvil – the IRA versus the British. He declared that the Protestants were Irish, and he devoted little thought to the question of what rights they might have: the way to solve the Irish problem was British withdrawal. The question of Unionist consent really did not come into it.

The two new chapters reveal new thinking. Now "peace in Ireland requires a settlement of the long-standing conflict between Irish nationalism and Irish Unionism. We cannot make peace without the Unionists. New relationships will have to be forged between all the people of our country."

Now it's about relationships rather than victories, about persuasion rather than force. He may be oversanguine in asserting that the consent of a majority of Unionists can be won for Irish unity if London and Dublin pressurise them enough: but the key point is that he is now thinking in terms of persuasion and diplomacy rather than force.

His book gives fascinating glimpses of stories yet untold about the peace process, including secret meetings with Catholic bishops and surreptitious contacts with the Irish government. Even while the violence was going on, Mr Adams was learning the diplomatic ropes and developing techniques which will stand him in good stead in the years of difficult negotiation which lie ahead. He has already shown more sureness of touch than, say, John Major.

The old hammer and anvil vision has gone. Now his message is that this is not a problem of military simplicities, but a multifaceted question. He has seen – as most Unionists have yet to grasp – that the issue has become irreversibly internationalised. The Unionists have to be taken into account, but so too do London, Dublin, Brussels and Washington.

The book opens in the 1960s with northern nationalists fatalistic, apathetic and politically feeble. It closes with Mr Adams and John Hume of the SDLP as two internationally fêted leaders, with no question of a return to second-class citizenship, and with the republicans united and *en route* to the political processes. Along the way it gives an insight into the development of the mind of the man who has led his people from the cul-de-sac of violence towards the path of peace.

The peace process had many twists and turns. In the Maze prison outside Belfast Ulster Volunteer Force prisoners rioted after the authorities moved in and confiscated mobile phones, drugs and other contraband. A substantial number of guns belonging to the small republican splinter group, the Irish National Liberation Army, were seized near Dublin.

The government began a fundamental review of policing requirements in the wake of the ceasefires.

John Major visited Londonderry, but plans for him to shake hands with Mitchel McLaughlin of Sinn Féin were dropped after republicans and police clashed in the streets. President Clinton, meanwhile, infuriated Mr Major by shaking hands with Gerry Adams, and by giving Sinn Féin permission to raise funds in the US.

The peace process moved on, too slowly for the republicans, too quickly for the British government. Another milestone was passed when a republican delegation, led by Martin McGuinness, met not just civil servants but a British minister, Michael Ancram, for the first time in more than two decades.

Mr Major had for some time declined to sanction such a meeting, saying he first wanted the republicans to move on the arms de-commissioning issue. Then the government announced that, following an exchange of letters with Sinn Féin, ''a sufficient basis'' for talks existed.

Megaphone diplomacy gives way to calm debate

The last time Martin McGuinness met a British minister, in 1972, he and other republicans were furtively spirited from Londonderry to London in conditions of the strictest secrecy. Some time ago he told the *Independent*: "I was on the run at the time. Six of us were taken in a blacked-out van from a back road in Derry to a field in which a helicopter landed.

"We were put in the helicopter and brought to the military end of Aldergrove airport near Belfast. We were then brought on by RAF plane to a military airfield in England, where we were met by a fleet of limousines. We were escorted by the Special Branch through London."

Yesterday, nearly two and a half decades on, the same Martin McGuinness led a Sinn Féin delegation, watched by a dozen camera crews, through Stormont's grandiose doors to meet Michael Ancram. Mr McGuinness's eyes are as flinty as ever, but the fair hair has become salt and pepper and he is now very much in negotiation mode.

After his 1972 encounter with Mr McGuinness, William Whitelaw wrote: "The meeting was a non-event. The IRA leaders simply made impossible demands. They were in a mood of defiance and determination to carry on until their absurd ultimatums were met." Mr McGuinness has this memory of that meeting: "All of us left quite clear in our minds that the British government were not yet at a position whereby we could do serious business." The republicans were flown back to Belfast and the war was stepped up.

Inside Stormont yesterday, the two sides who were deadly enemies talked on for more than four hours in a businesslike and non-confrontational fashion. The people in the meeting have had their brushes with death: Michael Ancram was in the Grand Hotel in Brighton when the IRA blew it up in 1984; Martin McGuinness says he has been "fired at by the British army on countless occasions".

But they shook hands briskly and got down to business. The two sides laid out their positions, which are still miles apart, but neither gave up and walked out in despair or angry protest. Outside the building their respective press officers chatted to the press and occasionally to each other.

Afterwards it emerged, in matter-of-fact fashion, that another meeting is to be arranged for next week. It has taken eight months to reach this point, and unless there are unexpected breakthroughs many more months of such contacts lie ahead. After the megaphone diplomacy of recent months, the meeting was a moment of slightly surprising calm.

Most of the important issues were touched on, but resolving them may take years rather than months. Round-table talks involving all parties also look months away but the bottom line is that both sides, and most of the other elements involved, fervently want the process to continue, and the guns to stay silent.

M artin McGuinness, who had become a frequent visitor to Stormont, is second only to Gerry Adams in importance in the republican movement.

---

13 MAY 1995   THE INDEPENDENT

Martin McGuinness: custodian of the republican conscience

T he last working day in Martin McGuinness's life which had any semblance of normality to it was 8 August 1971. He was working in his home city of Londonderry at the time, helping out with the pre-packed bacon in Doherty's butcher's.

The following day a wave of arrests heralded the introduction of internment without trial, and soon large-scale gun battles broke out in the city. After that Martin McGuinness never went back to the bacon counter, instead becoming a full-time street fighter.

Martin McGuinness talks to press and TV reporters after meeting NIO minister Michael Ancram at Stormont

For nearly a quarter of a century since then he has been regarded as personifying the leadership of the IRA: an implacable, relentless, ruthless, ingenious opponent of the British presence in Ireland, a man who will never, ever, accept that that presence could be legitimate.

Gerry Adams stands at the head of the republican movement, acting as its leader and chief strategist. Martin McGuinness has been his indispensable partner, his implicitly trusted associate, the movement's primary militarist and chief negotiator. Mr Adams may have been the principal architect of the IRA ceasefire, but it is almost certainly true that the cessation would not have come about without Mr McGuinness's wholehearted support.

Many in the republican movement, while greatly admiring Mr Adams, have always kept a wary eye on him. He was, they thought, maybe a little bit too much of a politician, a little bit too interested in dialogue, a little bit too prepared to compromise. But the presence at his side of Martin McGuinness served to still those fears. The Derry man's reputation as the hardline guarantor of the movement, the man who would never sell out the republican cause, who would never rest until the British were driven out, reassured almost all doubters.

99

His IRA credentials are certainly impeccable, and his personal style is legendarily direct. Yet there is more to Mr McGuinness than one half of the Adams–McGuinness soft-cop–hard-cop act. It is just that: something of an act. Mr Adams is not a straightforward dove, and Mr McGuinness is not just a straightforward hawk.

At a very early stage the IRA recognised his leadership potential. He joined in 1971 after spending some frustrating months in another republican group which proved not militant enough for his taste. By July 1972 he had, as they say in the IRA, "big stripes", and was important enough to be included in the delegation flown secretly to London to see William Whitelaw. He was 22 at the time: he and Gerry Adams, two years his senior, were the youngest of the group.

After the failure of the meeting he was soon on the run again, the newspapers describing him as one of Northern Ireland's most wanted men. He was, he said, "fired at by the British army on countless occasions". He was lucky to survive that period: many of his IRA associates did not.

His legendary commitment to the campaign of violence was all the more surprising in that he did not come from a family with a republican history: his mother fretted that he was losing out on his apprenticeship as a butcher. But he was from the Bogside, and he had been radicalised by the denial of civil rights.

In his words: "When people marched they were attacked and beaten by the RUC, who were acting at the behest of the Unionists. We saw our fathers and mothers humiliated like that, and we were not prepared to take it any more. Things changed. People decided they would struggle against what was wrong in this country."

The Derry IRA was noted in the early 1970s for wreaking havoc in the city centre, its relentless bombing campaign flattening a large number of buildings. It was also noted for causing fewer civilian casualties than the Belfast IRA. Eventually Mr McGuinness was arrested in the Republic, serving a couple of short jail sentences for IRA membership.

In the latter part of the 1970s he and Mr Adams were the two most prominent members of a group of northern militants who overthrew the southern-based old guard, headed by Ruairí Ó Brádaigh. They argued that the IRA was almost on its knees, and that in 1974–5 the old leadership had been tricked and fooled by the British into declaring what Mr McGuinness described as a disastrous ceasefire.

They accused the old leaders of seeking unrealistic short cuts, declared that talk of early British withdrawal was a mirage, and impressed on their supporters that the only way to get the British out was by stepping up the war. The war was indeed stepped up, and after the 1981 hunger strikes Sinn Féin was built up into a powerful political adjunct. It was during those hunger strikes that

100

the Adams–McGuinness relationship developed into one of absolute trust.

Ó Brádaigh broke with the Adams–McGuinness faction in 1986, warning that it was moving inexorably into politics. At that year's Sinn Féin *ard-fheis* Mr McGuinness made a decisive intervention, pouring scorn on the Ó Brádaigh faction: "They tell you that it is inevitable that the war against British rule will be run down. They deliberately infer that the present leadership of Sinn Féin and the IRA are intent on edging the republican movement on to a constitutional path. Shame, shame, shame. Don't walk away from the struggle. We will lead you to the Republic."

Today Ó Brádaigh, at the head of a tiny disgruntled group styling itself Republican Sinn Féin, is claiming that his warnings have been vindicated. The same men who accused him of an ill-judged ceasefire have themselves called not just a temporary halt but a permanent cessation. Many republicans have carefully considered Ó Brádaigh's arguments: the fact that they have not won widespread support is due in large measure to the confidence they have in Mr McGuinness.

Mr Adams and Mr McGuinness are committed to negotiation, with Mr McGuinness developing into the chief negotiator. He has shown himself to be much more than a simple soldier. He has also shown a pragmatic streak not evident in his early days on the streets of Derry.

The paradox and the conundrum is that Martin McGuinness, the custodian of the republican conscience, the man who will never accept the British presence, has now been up to Stormont half a dozen times. He knows the facts of political life: and the fact is that a united Ireland is not on the horizon.

He is astute enough to see that the rest of nationalist Ireland has accepted that Unionist consent is a prerequisite for a united Ireland and that this, to say the least, is unlikely to be forthcoming in the foreseeable future. Unless he is deluding himself, therefore, he must know that the course on which he has embarked is destined to end in a settlement based on compromise rather than victory.

On the old purist republican reading he, with Mr Adams, stopped the war short of victory. On another, they eventually came to see that the IRA's violent campaign, while it shook these islands for a quarter of a century, had run its course and was not advancing their aims.

If the second reading is correct, then Martin McGuinness is now, after all his years at war, committed to using his formidable reputation and talents to lead his people towards a peaceful path. The man who was once the guarantor of the armed struggle may have become a guarantor of peace.

In late May much of the Irish body politic, from north and south, flew to Washington for a major conference designed to interest US businessmen in investing in Northern Ireland. The event's commercial aspects were overshadowed by the first meeting ever to take place between Gerry Adams and Sir Patrick Mayhew.

26 MAY 1995   THE INDEPENDENT

A little bit of history in Suite 6006

The meeting here in Washington between Gerry Adams and Sir Patrick Mayhew may go down in Irish history as an event of great moment, but viewed from close up it had elements of both the mundane and the farcical.

It took place against the background of the White House-sponsored Irish trade and investment conference, which has brought across the Atlantic hundreds of business people, politicians and community workers.

Downstairs in the Washington Sheraton hotel they mingled at a series of receptions, one of them hosted by Sinn Féin. A lot of people have now met republican representatives for the first time, though the mainstream Unionist politicians who are here will have none of it. Peter Robinson of the Democratic Unionist party may have sat at a table adjoining that of Mr Adams, but the DUP deputy leader is exuding nothing but frigidity towards Sinn Féin. A historic handshake between the two is not in prospect. Upstairs, however, Mr Adams and Sir Patrick, who a year ago were at war with each other, were doing business.

The camera crews clustered around Suite 6006 awaiting the arrival of the two principals. Each time the lift doors opened the cameramen darted forward. Several times they found only startled Americans, some of whom were here for, appropriately enough, a gun convention, while others were attending a huge black gospel gathering: the hotel is on the scale of a medium-sized Northern Ireland town.

The camera crews produced a moment of farce when they pounced on one lift, only to find it contained more camera crews pouncing back at them. Then finally there was Sir Patrick, who was adamant that the historic handshake would take place behind closed doors. "Would you let one camera in," pleaded a photographer, "just one?" He would not. Two minutes later Mr Adams appeared with Richard McAuley, his press officer, and Mairead Keane, Sinn Féin's US representative. Entering the suite they found Sir Patrick with Tory MP James Cran and a note-taker. Everybody shook hands.

The Sinn Féin leader and the Northern Ireland Secretary did all the talking. Sir Patrick asked Mr Adams for movement on de-commissioning weapons; Mr Adams replied that he too wanted to see the gun taken out of politics. They cantered around the familiar course. No coffee was served. No jokes were made but there were no raised voices and no sticky moments. After a little over half an hour it ended with another round of handshakes. Mr Adams went outside to tell the clamouring cameras that it had been "a frank and friendly and positive exchange". The British party waited till he had moved on, then Sir Patrick emerged to say it had been civil rather than friendly.

Afterwards British and Sinn Féin press officers chatted to reporters in a corridor. Mr McAuley explained the approach taken by Mr Adams: "From the very beginning Gerry made a strong bid to engage at a personal level. We knew what they were likely to say: they knew what we were likely to say. We wanted to try to get just a wee bit beyond that by trying to get through to Mayhew. That's the first time the guy has talked to republicans, so here was an opportunity at a personal level to engage and to get this guy hopefully going away thinking, at the back of his head, that these people are human."

At this point an official from the British embassy in Washington overheard the Sinn Féin man saying the meeting had lasted 35 minutes. "Was it 35 minutes?" the official asked Mr McAuley. "Thirty-two, I made it, so I've said half an hour. No need to be that precise. Half an hour is what I'm saying." Mr McAuley nodded: "Right, there you are," he assented. They agreed to split the difference and call it half an hour.

Mr McAuley was a close friend of Mairead Farrell, the unarmed IRA woman shot dead by undercover SAS soldiers in Gibraltar. He wept when she died. The embassy official was the cousin of an SAS soldier shot dead by the IRA in Belfast in 1980. Yet here they were doing business of a sort in a Washington hotel. They were concerned with mundane details, yet it was a form of dialogue, and it was done civilly. The peace process is proceeding, with former sworn enemies working out in small ways how they can do business with each other.

In the improving atmosphere of peace,
new departures could now be
contemplated. One was the first formal
royal visit to Dublin since before partition.

2 JUNE 1995   THE INDEPENDENT

Prince taps vein of Anglo-Irish good will

Outside Dublin Castle, former seat of British rule in Ireland, a crowd of some thousands filed past, brandishing placards denouncing Britain in general and Prince Charles in particular.

Led by a figure of death, carrying a sickle and meant to represent Britain, they not only denounced British army actions during the Troubles, but went back 150 years to the Great Famine and even further to Oliver Cromwell.

Inside the castle, John Bruton, the Taoiseach, was declaring, to applause, that it was time to exorcise "certain memories that have lain between our two peoples like a sword". These two strikingly different reactions to this first formal royal visit for 80 years, illustrated conflicting but co-existing moods in Ireland. One, most distinct among republican and left-wing groups, is to dwell on the many hangovers of the Troubles. The other is the sense that the ending of violence has brought a real chance to make a historic new beginning.

Between these poles there are other tendencies, including indifference, personal curiosity about a prince who has had such an eventful personal life, and much of the traditional Irish instinct to welcome visitors from abroad. But in general Prince Charles has been received warmly and with enormous good will.

Relations between Britain and the Irish Republic have for a quarter of a century been particularly strained by the Northern Ireland conflict, but even before the Troubles they could never have been described as settled and normalised. The Republic's achievement of self-government in the 1920s ushered in a period of considerable coolness. British forces departed from Dublin following five years of often violent conflict, and the preceding negotiations had split the Irish into two factions which clashed in a brief but bitter civil war.

104

The southern state was born after a period of violence. Furthermore, the British stayed on in the six counties which became Northern Ireland, leaving an item of unfinished business which would later flare up.

Ireland's decision to remain neutral during the Second World War did nothing to improve Anglo-Irish relations. The fact that many thousands of Irishmen fought in the British army during the war was played down in the Republic and has only recently become the subject of public commemoration. The 1950s and 1960s brought a gradual thaw in London–Dublin relations. British ambassadors to Dublin spent less time listening to the legendary harangues from the Taoiseach, Eamon de Valera, on the immorality of partition and were able to spend more time on matters of trade and business.

The outbreak of the Troubles, however, brought new difficulties. The Irish staged a protest at the United Nations and at one point moved army guns and field hospitals up towards the border. After Bloody Sunday in 1972 a mob burnt down the British embassy in Dublin, and in Co Sligo in 1979 the IRA assassinated Lord Mountbatten, Prince Charles's great-uncle and close confidant. After these low points Anglo-Irish relations have improved, the two governments coming to regard Northern Ireland as a difficult common problem which was best managed jointly. The 1985 Anglo-Irish agreement, and more recently the Downing Street declaration and the framework document, were clear signs of this new partnership approach.

Viewed only in terms of politics and terrorism, Anglo-Irish relations can appear little more than a battlefield. At many other levels, however, relationships have not been sundered. Geography and history, combined with a common language and elements of common culture, have created strong bonds. Both countries are members of the European Union. Hundreds of thousands of Irish migrants have made their home in Britain, while thousands of British people live happily in Ireland. Because no one got round to changing the laws, the Irish need no passports to enter Britain and while there they can vote in British elections.

Irish personalities abound in British television, while everyone in the Republic watches British television and many read British newspapers. Terry Wogan commentates for Britain in the Eurovision Song Contest, while Jack Charlton is the hugely popular manager of the Irish football team. Many Irish people, including republicans, take a great interest in the British monarchy and, as this visit has shown, there is a great fund of good will which has survived all the traumas of the Troubles.

The contents of February's framework document had come as a body blow to the reputation of Ulster Unionist party leader James Molyneaux, who wrongly believed his "special relationship" with John Major would prevent anything unwelcome to Unionists.

In June Mr Molyneaux had an opportunity to recover some ground when the death of Popular Unionist MP Sir James Kilfedder caused a Westminster by-election. Though it first seemed an easy seat for the party to snap up, it quickly became apparent that the prize was slipping through the party's fingers.

---

9 JUNE 1995   THE INDEPENDENT

Rebel ready to take Unionism by storm

A tall figure, distinguished by his confident bearing and a shock of snow-white hair, dominated the entrance to the market in the seaside town of Bangor, Co Down.

By rights R.L. McCartney QC, known to everyone as Bob, should be an underdog in this by-election. He once had a short, controversial political career but he has been away from the mainstream for many years, and he is up against Northern Ireland's biggest political grouping, the Ulster Unionist party,

Yet events have conspired to make him favourite to take the seat, and in the process deliver a major shock to the Unionist political system. A McCartney success could precipitate a leadership crisis and launch a major reassessment of Unionism's future direction.

Bob McCartney QC on his way to winning the North Down by-election and delivering a shock to the Ulster Unionist system

In Bangor market Bob McCartney seemed genuinely delighted at his reception, as a series of passers-by wished him well and promised their support. He said: "They feel the Ulster Unionist party hasn't represented them, they need someone who can speak out rationally against nationalist propaganda."

He was standing next to a stall selling garden gnomes at £1.99 each. His projection is that the Unionist party is peopled by political pygmies who have not given real leadership, either to Protestants or to the many Catholics whom he argues quietly support the union with Britain.

The Unionist party is open to such attacks because its style, under James Molyneaux, is so resolutely low-key. It is also vulnerable because of its general performance over the past year, when it was caught off-balance first by the IRA ceasefire and then by the Anglo-Irish framework document.

107

It did not anticipate the republican cessation, and it was dismayed by the unmistakably green tinge of the framework document. As one veteran observer put it: "They still haven't adjusted to the new order of peace. They're still transfixed, like rabbits in a headlight."

The party leadership was rattled in the spring by the unexpectedly strong showing of a stalking-horse candidate who stood against Mr Molyneaux. Now this by-election has given Mr McCartney the opportunity to capitalise on grassroots dissatisfaction.

The Unionist party's attitude towards the contest has shown signs of complacency. One of the campaign co-ordinators took a week off for a holiday in the sun, while the choice of candidate has drawn much comment. The party passed over Reg Empey, who had a high profile as a former Lord Mayor of Belfast.

It chose instead Alan McFarland, who is by no means a poor candidate but who suffers the disadvantages of being a virtually unknown outsider with few obvious ties to the constituency. His selection automatically made Mr McCartney the frontrunner and the man to beat – the bookies have Mr McCartney as 1 to 3 and Mr McFarland as 7 to 2. One of the other minor candidates confided privately that he would not have bothered standing if Mr Empey had been chosen.

North Down is the richest of Northern Ireland's 17 Westminster constituencies and probably the least affected by the Troubles. No nationalist is standing in this largely Protestant area. It has some rundown housing estates, but to out-siders it is typified by "the gold coast" – a stretch of prime luxury homes overlooking Belfast lough.

Bob McCartney lives in one of the gold coast's most splendid houses, but was brought up in very different circumstances on Belfast's Shankill Road, one of the city's heartlands of both loyalism and deprivation. A grammar school boy, he qualified first as a solicitor and then as a barrister, becoming one of Northern Ireland's top QCs.

He famously burst onto the political scene in 1981, grabbing the microphone from a startled Rev Ian Paisley at a Unionist rally and denouncing him as a fascist. He was at first hailed as a hero come to rescue Unionism, with the ability to provide an alternative to the bombast of Mr Paisley and the lack of clarity of Mr Molyneaux. He seemed to offer many of the qualities which Unionist leaders lacked, including self-assuredness, proven success in a profession, and communication skills.

He joined the Ulster Unionist party but as time went on criticisms of his ap-proach mounted: he was said to be arrogant, impatient, abrasive and difficult to work with. At one stage he described Unionist MPs as "half-baked dodos". In the mid-1980s he switched policies from supporting devolution to advocating complete integration with Britain.

108

In 1987 he defied a party directive and stood in North Down against Sir James Kilfedder as a "Real Unionist" candidate. He came within 4,000 votes of winning, but was expelled from the party and his political career seemed to be over.

He is back with his legendary abrasiveness undiminished. The local *County Down Spectator* gave this account of a recent campaign debate: "Mr McCartney barely concealed his anger when a Conservative supporter interrupted his response on how he believed he would be listened to as an independent. Glaring from the platform, he told him that if he did not keep quiet he would tell the meeting some things the Conservative party would rather not have publicised."

Mr McCartney's career in politics began when he took on the Rev Ian Paisley but now, by a supreme irony, Mr Paisley is supporting him in this contest. Both argue that the framework document places the union in peril, and both want to damage the main Unionist party. The Paisleyite support is difficult to reconcile with Mr McCartney's vision of a new non-sectarian Unionist movement embracing both Protestants and Catholics. It is also difficult to see how one new MP could reverse the British government's settled approach of building up Anglo-Irish relations and opt instead for policies aimed at strengthening the union.

But those are questions for another day. More immediately, polling day on 15 June will provide an opportunity for Unionists to pass judgement on the main Unionist party and on what Bob McCartney characterises as its politics of drift and lack of direction.

POSTSCRIPT

Mr McCartney duly won the seat in a particularly low poll. His victory was yet another reflection on Mr Molyneaux's performance.

Ju ne brought the death of one of the noblest and most tragic figures of the Troubles, Gordon Wilson of Enniskillen.

Nobility among the rubble

After the 1987 Poppy Day explosion in Enniskillen two images flashed around the world. The first was the fact that an IRA bombing had killed 11 Protestant civilians as they gathered on Remembrance Day; the second was Gordon Wilson's almost superhuman display of Christian charity and forgiveness.

Mr Wilson and his daughter Marie, who was a nurse aged 20, were buried in rubble by the explosion. He survived and she did not. His broadcast account of lying in the debris holding her hand was one of the most poignant and affecting moments of the quarter-century of Irish Troubles.

Mr Wilson died in Enniskillen, Co Fermanagh, at the age of 67, after being suddenly taken ill.

He will go down in Irish history as the man who, after his daughter's death, recounted that her last words to him were: "Daddy, I love you very much." And he summoned the strength of character to add: "She was a great wee lassie. She was a pet, and she's dead. But I bear no ill will, I bear no grudge."

The savagery of the IRA bombers, the tragedy and futility of Marie Wilson's death, and Gordon Wilson's personal victory over bitterness mean that in Ireland the Enniskillen attack will never be forgotten. In the aftermath he received a special tribute from the Queen and was voted Man of the Year by the BBC's *Today* programme, ahead of Terry Waite and Mikhail Gorbachev. He said then with characteristic modesty: "I'm not worthy of it. The others are very important people. I'm not in their class. I'm just an ordinary guy."

Later he wrote a book called *Marie* and did what he could for the cause of peace. He attracted Unionist criticism in 1993 when he accepted an Irish government invitation to become a member of the Irish Senate, where he made a number of heartfelt contributions.

Some months later more controversy followed when he asked to meet the IRA, in the hope that a personal appeal might reach them. But he reported sadly: "They listened, but they made no change in their position. Perhaps it was naïve of me to imagine that because it was me they would. I went in innocence to search for what my heart told me might be a way forward. I got nothing."

By August 1994, however, the IRA campaign had ceased, and two months later Gordon Wilson sat alongside Sinn Féin representatives in the Forum for Peace and Reconciliation in Dublin. His forbearance and his appeal for continuing peace brought a standing ovation.

After Marie's death Mr Wilson said: "Don't ask me, please, for a purpose. I don't have a purpose. I don't have an answer. But I know there has to be a plan. It's part of a greater plan, and God is good."

In fact, Enniskillen can now with hindsight be described as one of the turning points of the Troubles. The deaths of Marie Wilson and 10 other people had crucial repercussions for republicans, for they put an end to Sinn Féin hopes of expansion, especially into the Irish Republic. An IRA spokesman admitted that the outer reaches of republican support were "just totally devastated".

The incident helped initiate a rethink within the IRA and Sinn Féin, and that in turn led to the debate which eventually produced last year's ceasefire. Over the past year Gordon Wilson may have had the comfort of reflecting that the tragedy of Enniskillen planted a seed which, years afterwards, helped his country move from war to peace.

Even at the height of the Troubles some tourists always came to Northern Ireland, but peace brought an influx of new visitors who were able to venture into previously hazardous areas.

---

7 AUGUST 1995   THE INDEPENDENT

Belfast tourist trail pulls no punches

Quite a few people turned to watch, and a number cheerfully waved, as our eye-catching open-topped bus passed up the Falls Road, cruising slowly to let the Americans on the top deck pan their video cameras across the IRA murals.

"There you can see the rising sun and the tricolour flags," Colin, the Citybus driver, pointed out as he paused at the memorial to "Freedom's Sons", the members of D company, 2nd battalion, Belfast Brigade of the IRA.

"And that's the gable wall of the Sinn Féin press offices," he continued. "The man on the mural is Bobby Sands. He was the first of 10 hunger strikers to die here in 1981. He died on hunger strike for political status for prisoners. He was also elected an MP in the British parliament." A man on a ladder with a paintbrush, touching up the huge depiction of a smiling Bobby Sands, nodded pleasantly towards the bus as the video cameras whirred. "Very friendly people throughout Belfast," remarked Colin.

In fact, if the number of smiles and waves the bus attracted was anything to go by, the Falls Road was the friendliest part of the whole city. Passers-by and people sunning themselves in their little gardens were noticeably cheerful and welcoming. This was, however, a warts-and-all tour. "If you look down onto the road surface," said Colin, "you'll see all the burn marks where the buses and vans and lorries were burnt out just a few weeks ago in the rioting after the release of Private Clegg."

The tour, called "Belfast – a living history", takes the tourists right through the republican and loyalist heartlands, pointing out not only the attractions of the city but also its notorious trouble spots. Colin, a driver with the publicly owned bus company, is genuinely proud of the place – "see how well our lovely city looks," he exclaimed at one point – but he also points out the scenes of bombings and shootings.

The contrast with what the same tour offered, just a year ago, was striking. A few weeks before the IRA ceasefire, the tourists were taken on a trip which not only skirted the violent areas but pretended they didn't exist. On a tour which lasted four hours the driver didn't once mention the war: not a word about the IRA or the UVF, not one reference to the Shankill or the Falls.

Today, however, visitors are offered a rounded picture. After the Falls the bus headed up the Shankill, Colin pointing out the Orange halls, the bunting, and the kerbstones painted red, white and blue. He slowed at the site of the old Ulster Defence Association headquarters, where 10 people died in an IRA bombing two years ago, pointed out the memorial to the dead, and commented: "It was a terrible atrocity, which I think brought both communities back together."

Outside the Rex bar three lads holding beer bottles gave the bus a cheer and a wave, but several men at work at a new Ulster Volunteer Force mural merely glanced round and remained engrossed in their work. The only hazards the tourist faced were a wee lad on the Shankill with a peashooter – "you always get the odd one," Colin remarked apologetically – and the low branches of trees sweeping the top of the bus.

112

At the end of the trip they applauded him and went off with their movies of Bobby Sands and the Shankill, things which are hopefully ceasing to be current affairs and are instead becoming the stuff of history.

It was not only foreign tourists who received a welcome up the Falls Road: so too did Protestants and Unionists from the other side of the peaceline.

11 AUGUST 1995   THE INDEPENDENT

Warm applause for Unionists in the lions' den

The 600-strong audience in Conway Mill, in the heart of the republican Falls Road, warmly applauded the strangest things. They clapped when speakers said the IRA had to de-commission its weapons and that prisoners who had killed could not expect to walk free from jail.

They applauded, at some length, the Protestant minister who declared: "I want to pay tribute to the folk who joined the Royal Ulster Constabulary to serve both communities, who paid the ultimate sacrifice and are dead."

The meeting had an Alice in Wonderland flavour. Many in the audience were members or supporters of Sinn Féin, who are more used to saluting the volunteers of the IRA: yet here they were clapping praise for the RUC.

But this was a new type of meeting, and one which showed the distance travelled since the IRA cessation of violence almost a year ago. It also showed how far there is still to go in the peace process. The panel, for a BBC *Question Time*-style session, consisted of Sinn Féin's Martin McGuinness, Mark Durkan of the Social Democratic and Labour party and Albert Reynolds, the former Fianna Fáil leader who was Taoiseach at the time of the ceasefire.

113

Most unusually there two Unionists, the Rev Ken Newell, and Roy Garland. Neither man is a significant political figure, but their very presence had huge symbolic significance in this republican lions' den, dominated by a huge portrait of IRA martyr Bobby Sands.

Each member of the panel was given a hero's welcome. Martin McGuinness got great applause when he outlined Sinn Féin's positions: no de-commissioning of IRA weapons, all-party talks now, release of prisoners and disbandment of the RUC.

Albert Reynolds too was given a great reception as he knocked the British government, as he has done repeatedly since he lost office, and supported the Sinn Féin line on de-commissioning, the release of prisoners, and talks. At the end he was besieged by well-wishers, hand-shakers, autograph-seekers.

But the applause for the Unionists when they voiced often directly contradictory views was by no means polite or perfunctory: on the contrary, it was warm and often prolonged. A series of speakers thanked them for coming.

On prisoners Mr Newell said: "I don't feel that people who have taken life and shed blood and devastated families for ever can simply walk out." On guns he said: "Unionists feel that if Sinn Féin do not get what they want out of round-table talks, there will be a return to violence."

A Conway Mill audience can surely never have heard anything like his tribute to the RUC before – still less react to it, as they did, with a warm round of applause. He was tackled from the floor on a number of points, though generally in a non-confrontational manner.

Speaking of the Unionist community, he had little immediate comfort to offer those seeking a loyalist De Klerk who would make a historic deal with nationalists. There were creative currents within Unionism, he said, but it would be three or four years before the Protestant community fully thought through its future. He summed up with a frankness the audience clearly found disarming: "I've been conscious of anger towards me as well as a welcome, and it's a funny feeling.

"We need to talk to each other: because we haven't been talking, a lot of pressure and anger and bad feeling has built up on both sides. I certainly feel there are enormous misconceptions, and the challenge for me is how you take this discussion out into the grassroots. We have to work out where to go together from here, because at the moment we're not friends, we haven't got the emotional bonding that we need if we're going to build a community that is worth living in. There's no future if we can't become friends."

The audience up the Falls Road, an area which has become an international byword for violence, again reacted with prolonged applause. The years of violence and isolation have left these people with a deep feeling of having been treated unfairly and unjustly by Unionism and by Britain. But they also displayed

114

other characteristics: tremendous hospitality and good humour, toleration and good will, and a palpable eagerness to reach out and enter dialogue with old foes.

The approach of the first anniversary of the IRA cessation brought assessments of how the two communities viewed life after a year of ceasefires.

12 AUGUST 1995   THE INDEPENDENT

Two perspectives on the peace

THE PROTESTANTS

After a year of ceasefires, Ulster Unionists are displaying a mixture of emotions which include apprehension about their political future, mistrust of the British government, suspicion about the IRA and Sinn Féin, and fear of any prospect of Irish unity.

This is unsurprising, given that such have been the Protestant preoccupations for more than a century. But overlaying those traditional concerns are new feelings: hope for the future, a tentative willingness to think of new departures, a readiness on the part of at least some to contemplate compromise. Above all, there is huge, palpable relief that the Troubles seem to be over.

A year on, there have still been no joyous celebrations in the streets: it wasn't that kind of war, and it's not that kind of peace. It looks and feels as though it's all over, but in Ireland no one can ever say with certainty that it might not break out again.

But the traditional wariness is being tempered with new hope, and the hope has grown steadily stronger as the peaceful months have passed. The IRA may still be out there, but the awful procession of funerals no longer dominates the nightly news. The peace is greatly appreciated, even though Unionist politicians

115

and thinkers have yet to provide their people with a coherent picture of how it came about, and how they should now react to it.

⌐The Rev Ian Paisley maintains that the IRA cessation is a trap and that Protestants now face "the worst crisis in Ulster's history", while the Ulster Unionist party regularly predicts that the IRA is itching to go back on the offensive.⌟

⌐But the clear consensus in the Protestant community as a whole is that the situation is one of opportunity rather than peril, with the past 12 months offering much evidence that the grassroots are much more upbeat than their political representatives.⌟

One very obvious sign of this lies within the loyalist paramilitary community, where newly emerged spokesmen such as David Ervine and Billy Hutchinson have taken a strikingly more conciliatory and open line than mainstream Unionist politicians.

One freshly painted mural on Belfast's loyalist Shankill Road features the traditional man with a gun, but today he stands under a slogan offering the choice: "Conflict or compromise". The underground loyalist groups still exist, but they are showing a genuine interest in politics and their ceasefire has, like the IRA's, been marked by a high degree of discipline.

The year brought a number of unwelcome developments for Unionists including the international fêting of Gerry Adams, but the protracted arms decommissioning dispute between the government and Sinn Féin helped reassure many that the republicans are not getting everything their own way.

Another major setback came with publication of the Anglo-Irish framework document in which London and Dublin set out a joint vision of the future which was far too green for Unionist tastes. The document brought no street protests, however, again suggesting that the grassroots have adapted to the post-ceasefire situation more easily than have their politicians.

Many sections of the Protestant community have been much more enthusiastic than their politicians. Businessmen, welcoming the new stability, are showing a pragmatic openness to new cross-border trading opportunities. Early unease among the predominantly Protestant members of the Royal Ulster Constabulary has been largely dispelled by government assurances that job losses are not imminent.

Tough political negotiations lie in the future, but since substantive talks seem to be more than a year ahead there is as yet no particularly sharp apprehension about what they could produce. When they do arrive, the question is whether some Unionist De Klerk will emerge to attempt a historic new deal, or whether the traditional stone wall will again be deployed.

In recent years the Protestant community has been in psychological retreat, alienated from the government, fearful of its long-term future and imbued with

116

the sense that it is inexorably losing out. Many of the factors which generated that angst are still present, but the ceasefires have markedly lifted communal morale, raised possibilities for a new beginning, and brought fresh cheer. This summer Protestants had two unwonted pleasures, the sun and the peace; and they have been basking and luxuriating in both.

THE CATHOLICS

Moderate Catholics see themselves as the real winners, the people who eventually persuaded the IRA to stop and who convinced Britain that Northern Ireland should be treated not as purely British but as an Anglo-Irish problem.

They believe they have won the major arguments, and set out a coherent and intelligent vision of Northern Ireland's future. Most of them believe that they do not yet live in a completely fair society, but think that steady progress is being made towards equality.

Their political leader, John Hume of the SDLP, is a respected international figure who played a key part in bringing about the IRA cessation. He also played a major role, both as a politician and as a theorist, in internationalising the Irish question and ensuring that it would no longer be treated as a British domestic problem.

Thus a community which until the 1960s was marked by impotence and internal divisions has been gradually transformed. It is now part of a political Internet, harnessing the power and influence of Dublin, Washington and Brussels. Long before the ceasefire it was a community on the way up, progressing not only politically but also in social and economic terms.

The ceasefire itself brought another leap in confidence for an already remarkably self-assured section of the population, which viewed republican violence as wrong-headed, outmoded and counterproductive. It now looks ahead to eventual political negotiations in which it believes the Unionists, and indeed the British, will be outclassed by Hume and the Irish government.

It will be seeking a far-reaching agreement which for the first time would include Sinn Féin in an all-inclusive settlement, a deal which would underpin the peace by offering something for everyone. The framework document, which outlined the intention of London and Dublin to create strong Anglo-Irish structures, were welcomed with quiet satisfaction.

From the start the general Catholic population was more ready than Protestants to believe that the IRA campaign was over for good, and readier to regard Sinn Féin as prodigals who had genuinely reformed and were to be welcomed into society.

Because of this belief Catholics in general have, like the Irish government, favoured a much faster pace in the peace process and want to see movement on issues such as the early release of prisoners. They favour an active and dynamic process to bring Sinn Féin into the mainstream as quickly as possible.

Their chief area of concern, in fact, is that the British government, by moving too slowly, could fatally damage the credibility of Gerry Adams with hardline republican elements who might then conclude that the peace process was a waste of time.

This fear has created much exasperation and irritation with the government, which moderate Catholics tend to hold in low regard and routinely criticise as a lumbering, ponderous, ill-coordinated and often unintelligent machine.

Within the republican community, that one-third of the Catholic population who regularly vote for Sinn Féin, things are more complicated. There the British are suspected of having more sinister motives, principally of hoping to split the republican movement so that the violence could restart and allow Britain the opportunity of achieving a military solution.

Such mistrust of Britain is endemic within republicanism, and Gerry Adams and other Sinn Féin leaders often accuse the government of bad faith and ulterior motives. The slow pace of the process over the past year has led to many grumbles, with the stalemate on the arms de-commissioning issue causing Adams to warn of an impending crisis.

But although there is much impatience there is no real sign, even within the hardline republican ghettos, of any significant body of opinion favouring a return to the war. That is not to say, however, that a handful of determined men might not appear somewhere and attempt to start the conflict again; and there is always the possibility of even minor bush fires spiralling out of control.

The IRA cessation has been surprisingly well disciplined, but in a land so suffused with paramilitarism the process will always require careful management. The general Catholic mood, however, is not conducive to a resumption: it is one of thankfulness and relief that the guns have fallen silent, and of hope for the future.

The marching season is often a tense time, and 1995 was no exception. Disturbances at a major Orange demonstration at Portadown, Co Armagh, in July were followed by trouble in Belfast and Londonderry in mid-August.

The momentum of the peace process, meanwhile, had been appreciably slowed by the dispute over de-commissioning, which dragged on for many months without resolution. All these factors combined to give a sense that the process had grown a little more shaky.

14 AUGUST 1995   THE INDEPENDENT

Thorns in the side of peace

The violent scenes at the marches in Northern Ireland during the weekend of 12–13 August raise questions about the state of health of the peace process. No one has been killed for almost a year: the guns have stopped and the bombs no longer go off. Most people now regard a return to violence as all but unimaginable, each passing day making a revival of terrorism less and less likely.

Yet the ancient art of coat-trailing seems as popular as ever. The parades were only the latest in a series which has disturbed the peace as both loyalists and republicans display an insatiable appetite for staging demonstrations which can lead to trouble.

The results, by Northern Ireland standards, are comparatively minor, in that no one has been killed or seriously hurt in the sporadic clashes. But each episode of street disorder adds another little layer to the patina of communal bitterness and tensions, and sets back any movement towards reconciliation.

The peace process has been buffeted, in its short life, not only by march controversies but by developments such as the early release of Private Lee Clegg, a change of government in the Irish Republic, and the protracted stalemate on de-commissioning weapons.

But although Gerry Adams and other republican leaders have often used the word crisis when berating the government for its alleged sluggishness, the ceasefires have at no stage really looked like breaking down. Because of this, and because most people hope so fervently that it will last, many have come to take the peace for granted.

Mr Adams and his close lieutenants can see the damage the republican movement would do itself by reverting to the gun: all their new-found friends and allies in Ireland, America and elsewhere would turn their backs and consign Sinn Féin to Arctic isolation.

But not everyone in the republican community thinks in such broad political terms, such as the man who called out "Bring back the IRA" as Mr Adams was speaking at a republican rally. Out there in the grassroots some argue that, a year on, Sinn Féin has not been fully admitted to the political processes; that Unionism looks unreconstructed and unyielding; that the only prisoner released has been Private Lee Clegg; and that Britain can never be trusted.

The British concentration on de-commissioning, it can be argued, is a sign that London's goal is a military victory over the IRA, and not the all-inclusive political settlement which Sinn Féin wants.

At the moment much attention is focused on Patrick Kelly, an IRA prisoner in an English prison who is suffering from skin cancer, and who republicans allege is being denied proper treatment. A republican declared at a meeting in Belfast this week: "For a lot of people in our community the whole peace process is a very abstract thing. If you're talking about tangible, concrete measures that would consolidate and move the thing forward, the issue of prisoners is one that can be easily identified and easily measured. To have seen no response from the British government is not only very disheartening, it's making people very angry and very frustrated. If we can't get treatment for Patrick Kelly for skin cancer, what does that say about the British government's approach to the broader issues?"

The Kelly case will presumably be dealt with at some stage, and at some stage an understanding on de-commissioning will emerge to allow the peace process to move on. But prisoners, guns and when inter-party talks should start are all issues which will remain thorny problems not for months but for years ahead.

Disputed marches and demonstrations will also continue. They have been taking place for a century and more, long before Northern Ireland even came into being, and have always been part of the background static. For example, it takes Bob Purdie a dozen pages, in his book *Politics in the Streets* (on the background to the civil rights agitation), to outline the large and small controversies and disturbances of the peace in the early 1960s. Many now hazily remember this as something of a golden age of peace and progress: in fact there were dozens of cases of riots, arson, and street clashes.

Such activities predated the quarter-century of terrorism, and show no sign of abating now. So while the republican and loyalist ceasefires are holding, the fact is that years of controversy lie ahead, both in politics and on the streets.

So far the clashes have been relatively contained, with brief outbursts of violence quickly dying away. The problem is that either a major political issue, or some small piece of street theatre, could escalate into something really threatening.

The ceasefires have brought encouraging little thaws in community relations with, for example, two Unionists venturing up the Falls Road to share a platform with Sinn Féin (*see* "Warm applause for Unionists in the lions' den", pp. 113–15). But a year of peace has led to little or no increase in trust between the two key components, the republicans and the government, and much of the discourse between them continues to be conducted by means of megaphone.

A government source said privately: "The feeling is that if [the peace] does make it through the 12-month barrier, it's going to be very difficult to unravel it." Irish nationalists, by contrast, worry about British complacency and argue that it's more complicated than that. One Dublin source said: "The ceasefires are a dynamic: you need a certain dynamism to hold them and they have to be underpinned by political negotiation. The fact that they are so popular doesn't necessarily mean that they are therefore irreversible. We can't rely on the threat of public anger to keep violence permanently off the screen: I don't think it has ever worked like that before."

In other words, the price of peace will be eternal vigilance – the most careful handling of all the minor dramas which might turn into a real crisis. Above all, critical judgements have continually to be made about the state of play within both republicanism and loyalism, and a watch kept for the rise of any new hawkish elements.

A genuine worry for many of the other participants in the peace process is the level of competence displayed by the government. Both nationalists and loyalists profess themselves puzzled by shifts in policy and baffled by the timing of some decisions. Generalised praise for John Major's personal commitment to peace is often accompanied by charges of inept day-to-day management of the process.

Everyone – including republicans – would be happier if London held to a more consistent line and displayed more sureness of touch in its treatment of what, a year on, is a delicate process which will continue to require judicious, intricate handling if it is to lead to lasting peace.

> **M**any people, meanwhile, were
> wondering how the army was passing its
> time in the absence of bullets and bombs.

Army retreats into world of virtual reality

S hortly after noon yesterday a man wearing a combat jacket and a balaclava hood tossed a home-made hand grenade at a British army Land Rover as it passed through O'Neill Square in Belfast. The missile exploded close to the vehicle. Shortly afterwards a soldier in a nearby street detained a man who was about to ride off on a motorcycle, while other troops were involved in a scuffle with youths.

No one was injured in the incident: no one could have been, for it did not really happen. There is no O'Neill Square in Belfast and there was no grenade attack, except as depicted on the screen of a normally restricted building in the Ballykinler army camp in peaceful Co Down.

In the absence of real bombs and bullets, the army has now resorted to combating virtual terrorism. The Falls Road may be reasonably quiet these days, but in Ballykinler camp the virtual shootings and bombings go on as soldiers rehearse dealing with any fresh outbreak of Troubles. The previously secret training facilities were thrown open to the media yesterday as the army sought to provide answers to the frequent enquiries about how, nearly a year after the IRA and loyalist ceasefires, 17,500 regular and locally recruited troops occupy themselves.

The army is much less in evidence on the streets and has become a rarity in many areas, but troop levels have been reduced by less than 1,500 during the past year. According to Brigadier David Strudley, the fact that the terrorists still retain their weapons and explosives, and are still targeting and training, means it is essential to maintain its present level of readiness.

While waiting for any new outbreak of violence, troops are mainly occupied in training, including that in the Invertron computer simulation hall. Several

122

dozen soldiers can sit at individual desks role-playing as a large screen displays Belfast street scenes. They have to imagine themselves as, for example, radio operators urgently calling an operations room to report an attack on their patrol. The sound effects, including loud explosions and confused shouting, can be deafening, while additional atmosphere is generated by thick smoke which is blown into the room. It all adds up to a high-tech and highly realistic computer game.

The Invertron also provides training in military techniques for use outside Northern Ireland. The soldiers are given maps and binoculars to study a country scene on the large screen. When they come under simulated machine-gun fire their job is to reply with mortar fire on to the enemy.

This is just a small part of an expanded training programme which has been made possible by the ending of the killings and the consequent reduction in street duties. With patrolling reduced to a quarter of what it once was, there is scope for more local training and for dispatching units to exercises in Cyprus and Gibraltar. There is also more emphasis on community relations work, such as constructing a river rescue facility and building a new footbridge in a scenic area of Co Antrim. In military jargon these are designated MACC tasks (military aid to civil community).

Air crews said they now have time for more rescue work. A Wessex helicopter pilot noted that the recent increase in tourist numbers meant more people were getting into trouble on cliff walks and getting lost in the Mourne mountains. After a year of peace, it seems tourism is causing the army more immediate problems than terrorism.

The anniversary of the IRA cessation was the occasion for a review of the year and a look at future prospects.

The scars of war and the path to reconciliation

Not forgotten: a British Legion wreath left in August 1995 at Warrenpoint, where 18 soldiers died in an IRA attack in August 1979

Northern Ireland has peace, but not quiet. There are no bombs but there is not yet reconciliation; it is many months away from full-scale political talks, and years away from agreement. The shooting may have stopped but the punishment beatings and intimidation continue. Protestant and Catholic extremists throw crude petrol bombs at each other's homes and places of worship. Peace walls still scar the face of Belfast.

Hopes for a dynamic, fast-moving peace process have faded as politicians bicker, and as the government and the republicans remain locked in the de-commissioning impasse. The pace of the peace process has also been impeded by the related questions of all-party talks.

These issues have created a stark fault-line within the process. On one side are the government and Unionist politicians, saying guns must be handed in before round-table talks can start. On the other side, arguing that this is unrealistic, are Sinn Féin and most nationalist politicians. Along with them, most unusually, are the loyalist paramilitary groups, who on this issue take a similar line to Sinn Féin.

The arms question has not totally stopped progress, but it has developed into a central defining issue – slowing everything down, preventing the development of momentum and mutual confidence among the participants, and causing considerable strains within the republican movement.

These strains appear to represent the greatest potential threat to the process. On the one hand, the security force assessment is that republican leaders remain committed to peace. Sir Hugh Annesley, Chief Constable of the RUC, said recently: "I believe from all the intelligence available to me that the leadership of the Provisionals wants the peace to continue."

He added, however, that there were "significant pockets of resistance" to the peace. The signs are, therefore, that Gerry Adams is engaged in holding off the hard men as he presses the government to move towards talks without de-commissioning.

The IRA statement which called off their campaign declared that "a solution will only be found as a result of inclusive negotiations". Twelve months later, any such negotiations still seem a long way off, leading Mr Adams to argue that this has created a dangerous political vacuum.

These pressures will continue and probably intensify unless some compromise formula can be found on the arms issue, as Mr Adams seeks to convince sceptics in the IRA that politics is preferable to terrorism. With factors such as these at work the peace process can never be regarded as completely safe and sound.

A year ago the IRA's announcement of a complete cessation of violence was not greeted with celebrations in the streets: it was accompanied by too many unanswered questions, and many uncertainties remain. Problems lie ahead as far as the eye can see.

But 100 or so people who, in the normal barbaric course of events, would be dead are still alive; and there is every reason to believe that with luck, ingenuity and careful judgement, the killings will not start again.

"My friends and I go down to Botanic Park in the evenings and wander around," said the middle-class 16-year-old girl from peaceful south Belfast. "It's all mixed and there's no trouble, but even so if you saw a friend and they had a Catholic name you wouldn't shout their name across the park. You'd be worried somebody would pick on them and they might get hit, you know, beaten up. You just have to be careful like that. Even though there's a military ceasefire there's not a ceasefire of other sorts."

Although peace may have arrived in Northern Ireland many ancient quarrels remain unresolved and there is still a lot of bigotry about. As the teenager's comment shows, there are a lot of unwritten rules which are well understood and have to be carefully observed. Most of these things are pretty much invisible to outside observers, who look at Belfast city centre and imagine they see people mixing freely and in an apparently relaxed fashion, enjoying the sun and the benefits of peace. The ceasefires have certainly lightened the atmosphere in many ways, but the basic sectarian grammar remains untouched.

The most obvious changes over the past year have been the sudden cessation of shootings and bombings and the consequent easing of security force activity. Police officers no longer have to check under their cars each morning for Semtex boobytrap devices, and in their Land Rovers they no longer need fear rocket or mortar attacks.

Shoppers no longer have to worry whether parked cars have bombs concealed in the boot, undergo searches on entering stores, or endure traffic queues as their vehicles are checked. Most city and town centres no longer have barriers to keep out the bombers. Parking is easier, and the black-uniformed civilian searchers have been paid off. In most areas soldiers have disappeared off the streets.

Tourists have replaced troops. There always were some holiday visitors, even at the height of the Troubles, but now many more are in evidence. There are back-packers aplenty, lots of foreign student types and some older couples. Not everyone in Northern Ireland was prepared for the influx, and not all the tourists know what to expect. On Sundays some can be seen wandering around the city centre unsuccessfully looking for something – anything – that is open, apart from churches. In a home bakery lately a French couple could be seen vainly seeking croissants, and being baffled by soda farls and Belfast baps.

But the locals have been surprisingly welcoming, and from the Republic have poured thousands of visitors, many of them crossing the border for the first time. Many shops now carry the sign "Pounds for punts", signifying they accept southern currency. There has also been a new flow in the other direction, with many Protestants venturing south to explore a country they previously avoided. Southern hoteliers and guest houses report a stream of what a Galway hotelier described as "a type of northern visitor we have not seen before".

The biggest changes to life styles have taken place in the hardline ghettos, for example in the tough areas of west and north Belfast whose streets were always the most violent of all. There is no longer heavy military patrolling here:

on the Falls Road last week, for example, four policemen could be seen sauntering along without tunics, flak jackets or military escort.

But the ghettos are still ghettos, with high unemployment, an often demoralised community and a large proportion of young men in prison. The ceasefires have made a great improvement but many problems remain and economic and political alienation persists.

The ceasefires have meant that some roads which used to be blocked off are now open again, at least during daylight hours, but formidable peaceline walls still crisscross the city. Most people accept that they will be there for years; some predict they will be there for ever.

Belfast's own brand of apartheid, much of it voluntary, has been in operation for decades and looks set to last for decades more, for there is segregation, in varying degrees, in most schools and many districts and work places. The segregation existed before the Troubles but was made much worse by them, and will be a continuing feature of life. With the ceasefires a start has been made on the road towards a more conventional existence and for most, life has brightened appreciably, but the old divisions will be a long time dying.

It's easy to come away with the impression that the security forces are in two minds about the IRA and loyalist ceasefires which have brought a year of comparative peace to Northern Ireland.

On the one hand, signs of relaxation are everywhere: an army base in the Falls has been bulldozed, roads reopened, parking restrictions eased. The civilian search unit has been disbanded, and security road checks have been reduced dramatically. Brightly coloured Panda cars are now to be seen in many parts of Belfast and there are more speed traps as the RUC has more time to devote to duties such as traffic. Army patrols are down by 75 per cent.

Last week half a dozen members of the Royal Irish Regiment were pictured in the Belfast *Irish News* handing over a charity cheque: they were shown fullface, something which would have been unthinkable a year ago because of the fear of IRA assassination.

Yet on a deeper level little has changed in the security posture. The combined complement of army and RUC has in a year been reduced by only 1,500 from 32,000 to 30,500. Some hundreds more troops may be withdrawn this autumn, but those who are pulled back to England remain under the command of the Northern Ireland GOC, ready to be recalled at short notice.

The guard, the authorities are anxious to point out, has not been dropped: there is no chance, they say, that a sudden return to violence would catch them on the hop. This high state of readiness means that the peace is being policed by the same security apparatus which until last August was coping with almost 100 terrorist deaths a year.

This machine keeps itself occupied in various ways. First, the IRA and the loyalist terrorist groups are still in existence and according to the authorities, continue to be engaged in training, targeting and other activities. The army and police are still watching this carefully, though the number of house searches, arrests and charges has fallen steeply.

Second, there are the normal civil policing duties needed in any society. Third, life in post-ceasefire Northern Ireland is by no means uneventful. In the last six months there have been around 60 arson attacks on Protestant and Catholic buildings and homes, dozens of paramilitary punishment beatings and an increase in the drugs trade.

In addition, controversial marches are a recurring problem: most pass off without incident, but if things go wrong there can be widespread disorder. The serious street disturbances in the month of July alone cost the RUC almost £2 million, the authorities say.

Even so, life has obviously eased considerably for the army and police. The army has much more time to devote to training and occasional overseas exercises, and has increased community relations work with youth groups and other organisations. The bomb disposal unit, which once dealt with 37 terrorist incidents a week, is now untroubled by paramilitary activity.

When the ceasefire was announced there was widespread speculation that many RUC officers and soldiers in the locally recruited Royal Irish Regiment would face redundancy. In the event, there have as yet been no such job losses. The army says there is no review of the RIR under way, while Chief Constable Sir Hugh Annesley speaks of force reductions as a very faraway prospect, saying that in the event of prolonged peace "clearly there will have to be, in the distant future, some down-sizing". The force is, however, no longer operating at full stretch and is now saving £1 million a month in overtime.

Meanwhile the government, looking to the longer term, is working on a white paper on policing. Internal reviews are considering what type of policing structures would be best suited to lasting peace. The Northern Ireland political parties – and the Irish government – will want a say in the shape of future policing, but since inter-party negotiations are not on the immediate horizon debate will not be fully joined for some time.

Sinn Féin asserts simply that the RUC is not an acceptable police force: other nationalist sources, while less antagonistic to the force, have nonetheless heavily criticised it. Unionist politicians tend to be protective of the RUC, regarding it as an institution to be defended rather than radically reformed.

In the short term the security forces are being kept in a high state of readiness: changes clearly lie ahead, but all the signs are that they will take much longer than was initially assumed. In the longer term there will be protracted and difficult debates on how such a divided society can best be policed.

A year after the IRA ceasefire, the economy seems poised for a period of expansion and improvement as the benefits of peace feed through the system. Apart from tourism, where the numbers of visitors have suddenly shot up, no huge financial peace dividend has appeared in the past 12 months. There are clear signs, however, of increased interest among potential investors. One example of this is the arrival of the British supermarket giants Sainsbury and Tesco, both of which are now moving in to open stores in the wake of the ceasefires.

The government and local analysts hope they will be joined by major manufacturing concerns who were in the past frightened off by the violence. The hope is also that local entrepreneurs, released from the worry of having their businesses blown up, will now have more confidence to expand. But even though a full year has passed since the IRA ceasefire the economy is only gradually being affected by the peace.

The central question lies in how to transform an economy deeply scarred by the Troubles into one which can compete successfully with the rest of Europe and other regions of the UK. It currently survives on huge subsidies from Britain, but even so it has particularly high unemployment and a number of black spots where jobs are pretty much a rarity.

On the credit side, the experts say the economy has performed surprisingly even against the background of the Troubles, and point out that in many areas workers and management kept going right through the worst of the violence. Battle-hardened firms which weathered so much will, they say, now come into their own.

A number of areas of potential growth are now opening up. Most immediately, tourists have already been flocking in from Britain, the Republic and further afield, with holiday visitors up by more than 50 per cent.

The prospects for more inward investment are now obviously immeasurably brighter. In the United States, in particular, the Clinton administration is making unusually determined efforts to coax American businesses to consider investing in Northern Ireland. Visits by potential investors are up by nearly 40 per cent.

Thousands of visitors from the Republic who never dared venture north are now exploring it for the first time, a strong indication of the potential for increased cross-border activity. North–south trade is artificially low, and business and commercial organisations are now placing great emphasis on the opportunity for increased commerce.

The official pitch to potential investors now says: "Our crime rate is low, our air is clean, our fields are green, our roads are uncongested, our housing is great value for money. We have 70-plus golf courses, many of championship standard and without queues."

None of that is an exaggeration, but the more thoughtful observers make the point that more will be needed if Northern Ireland is to reach its full potential. The paramilitary ceasefires have brought peace, but full stability will not be achieved until they have been underpinned by a political settlement.

Doug Riley, head of British Telecom in Northern Ireland, said as chairman of the local CBI: "I am strongly of the view that if there is no political movement we will not achieve the success that we deserve on the economic front. People will hold back until we have in place the frameworks and structures which we can all recognise, respect and work with, and which can manage inward investment and deal with American and European interest."

But such sentiments have proved controversial. The fact that business figures have been urging political dialogue and movement towards a settlement, as well as encouraging more cross-border activity, has drawn angry reaction from loyalist politicians.

Democratic Unionist MP Peter Robinson, for example, attacked commercial figures as "a band of business bloodsuckers, moneyed muck-worms and government lickspittles". There have also been loyalist protests about the government's policy of increasingly directing resources towards the most deprived areas, which tend to be largely (though by no means exclusively) Catholic.

Such exchanges demonstrate the gulf which exists between Unionist politicians and much of the business community, illustrating the gap between those who regard the ceasefires with deep suspicion and those who see them as a moment of opportunity.

There is still much uncertainty: the ceasefires might not last, and if they do jobs in the security sector will be lost. But most of those concerned seem to be operating on the assumption that peace is here to stay and that the economy's prospects are bright.

It can be all too easy to overlook the tragic legacies of the Troubles, the lasting human costs of a quarter of a century of conflict and 3,500 deaths. The deaths may have stopped, but 25 brutal years have left behind hundreds of widows and other bereaved for whom peace has a bittersweet flavour. Many remain bitter, though some have displayed almost superhuman qualities of reconciliation and forgiveness.

The fading of terrorism, while welcome to everyone, has left much unfinished business. Many of the bereaved feel a sense of political as well as personal grievance, sometimes towards the authorities and sometimes towards the paramilitary groups.

The IRA and the loyalist terrorists killed thousands of people and injured many thousands more, inflicting physical and mental scars on an untold number of families. Paramilitary beatings and enforced exiles continue: there must be hundreds of people, living in England, Scotland or further afield, who feel unable to return home.

Much attention has centred recently on "the disappeared" – the dozen or more people who vanished in the 1970s and are assumed to have been killed and secretly buried by the IRA. Relatives are now coming forward to appeal for information about the location of their bodies so they can be exhumed and given proper burials.

A number of relatives have broadcast heart-rending appeals, particularly in the case of Jean McConville, a widow who was abducted in the Falls Road district in 1972 and never heard of again. Her family of 10 children was wrecked and broken up by her disappearance, with the children taken into care. The mental torment of those children, who have spent 23 years in the grief of assuming their mother was dead, but of not knowing for sure, can only be guessed at.

There are also persisting complaints against the security forces, particularly concerning some of the 300 cases in which people were killed by soldiers. The relatives of many of those shot feel their killings were unjustified. Like the relatives of the disappeared, they too are pressing for more information and fresh investigations.

Others live in hope that their nightmares might some day end. Bernard Kane, who is 64, suffers from angina, deafness and a nervous disability. His wife has a brain tumour. Their 37-year-old son Patrick is in prison for the murders of two army corporals shot dead by the IRA when they drove into a republican funeral in 1988.

Patrick Kane was at the funeral but was not present when the soldiers were killed. He was nonetheless given a life sentence in a case which has been taken up by the Irish government, the Catholic church, the Labour party and human rights organisations.

Bernard Kane recently received prolonged applause when he stood up at a public meeting in west Belfast and, with quiet dignity and eloquence, appealed for support for his son's case. He said yesterday: "I don't find speaking like that easy. I be wrecked for days afterward with the old nerves. It's not a thing that comes easy to me but I know I have to do it, for Patrick's sake.

"He's doing great in jail. They've given him two hearing aids and it's opened up a whole new world for him. His hearing was very bad since he was a child, he was always in a remedial class in school. In there he's learnt to read and write, and it's wonderful the change it's made in him. Our Pat was a very introverted person but now he's much more confident. The authorities say they will review his case in 1997 but we need him out now. We want him out while his mother and myself are still around to see him."

On the ceasefire anniversary itself
Belfast reflected on the moment but
displayed little outward emotion.

1 SEPTEMBER 1995   THE INDEPENDENT

Ulster tiptoes to a new future

Catching them young: the junior section of a loyalist band in Belfast

Belfast yesterday marked and commemorated the year of peace but did not celebrate it. The city registered that, against the expectations of many, the ceasefire had lasted a full 12 months; but still nobody danced in its streets.

Instead it was for some a day of prayer, for the politicians a day of reiterating familiar positions, a day of hope for some that their children would know peace, but a day of cynicism for others.

Many of those who were unconvinced when the IRA announced its complete cessation are still unconvinced that it can last. Yesterday there was, if anything, more uncertainty about the peace process than there was a year ago. Those who believed it would unlock the door to a new era of dialogue and progress have experienced disillusionment as the impasse over de-commissioning of arms has dragged on.

Sir Patrick Mayhew again urged republicans to de-commission arms so that round-table talks could begin, while Martin McGuinness of Sinn Féin insisted the IRA would regard the hand-over of a single weapon as an act of surrender. Each accused the other of inflexibility.

Judged by such political exchanges, the peace process evidently lacks momentum and is inching rather than striding along, with little development of mutual confidence or trust. For many it is too much of an abstract process: in the republican ghettos frustration is expressed that Sinn Féin is still not in all-party talks, and that no prisoners have been released.

There is still much sectarianism and bitterness out there, with arson attacks on Orange halls and Catholic church property. The marching season's repeated disturbances were a sobering reminder that, Troubles or no Troubles, coat-trailing and territorial disputes will continue.

Those marches shook the confidence of many who had assumed, perhaps complacently, that the public popularity of peace meant that war could not return. The street confrontations gave a glimpse of a scenario in which a chain of minor incidents could, if allowed to escalate, conceivably threaten the entire process.

That possibility remains, yet there is much more to it than the ritual political incantations and the sound of belligerently marching feet. Beneath the surface there are many little signs of some thaws in the permafrost – meetings, many unpublicised, across the divide and across the border, personal relationships being built up, people venturing out of their shells.

The same Gerry Adams who complains that the process is in crisis has, during the year, shaken hands with Sir Patrick Mayhew, his deputy Michael Ancram, Bill Clinton, Nelson Mandela and every major nationalist politician in Ireland. Most of these are people who believe in Sinn Féin's new-found commitment to politics.

Most Unionist politicians, by contrast, affect not to believe a word of it. Their role during the process has been to stay out of it and urge the government to end it. This view was reflected by the Unionist Lord Mayor of Belfast, Eric Smyth. Speaking live on Ulster Television, in front of a city hall conspicuously free of any ceasefire celebrations, Mr Smyth said: "There's no celebration because nobody believes in it. The British government has given in to the IRA, giving them concessions after concessions, and Gerry Adams threatens every time that the peace process is going to fall down if they don't get what they want.

"I don't believe the vast majority of people in Northern Ireland believe that there is a peace process. Yes, we've enjoyed peace as such and nobody's getting killed, but there is still racketeering, beatings and burnings. The IRA's bottom line is a united Ireland, so what happens when they realise they're not going to get that? I think they will return if they don't get their goal of a united Ireland."

This scepticism is shared by many in the Protestant community, which helps explain why an ecumenical thanksgiving service in the city's St Anne's Church of Ireland cathedral was attended by fewer than 200 people. But the point was made, in another part of the city, that there has already been a peace dividend.

In Shaftesbury Square a neon sign scrolled through the names of the thousands of people who have died. Almost 100 of those people met their violent deaths in the 12 months leading up to the ceasefire: since then only three have been added to the list. Thus the peace process has ensured that almost 100 people, who might otherwise be dead, are alive to hear the Lord Mayor tell them that the whole thing has been a waste of time.

For many months the peace process was dogged by the de-commissioning issue, with both the republicans and the British government refusing to give way. It was widely assumed, however, that an Anglo-Irish summit scheduled for early September would come up with a formula which could break the deadlock.

But the summit was called off at the last moment when the two governments could not agree. It was a tense moment as the de-commissioning issue suddenly seemed to have the capacity to make or break the entire process.

Cultural differences lead to political log jam

Behind the London–Dublin disagreement lie fundamentally differing perceptions about the nature of the Irish peace process and the bona fides of the republican movement. The absence of accord is caused as much by cultural and psychological divergences as by political outlook.

The differences have crystallised in the de-commissioning issue which is now imposing ever-greater strains on the process, and has developed into the most serious political problem encountered in the year since the IRA cessation of violence.

While Britain holds that the ceasefire itself is not enough to start movement to all-party talks, and that actual de-commissioning of weaponry is necessary, the Dublin view is that it is unrealistic to expect any hand-over from the IRA.

The key underlying judgement here is how much confidence is to be placed in Gerry Adams and the republican leaders who engineered the ceasefire. Recently the Taoiseach, John Bruton, a long-time bitter opponent of the republicans, declared publicly that he trusted the leaders of Sinn Féin. No British minister is likely to make any such comment.

The British strategy has been to test the republican commitment by pushing ever harder on the de-commissioning issue, and to maintain the process at a slow and cautious pace. Dublin, by contrast, had much more confidence in the republicans from the start.

Dublin has been surprised by the way London has increased and maintained the emphasis on de-commissioning. A year ago an Irish source said privately that pushing de-commissioning would be a suitable tactic if the British wanted "to give [the republicans] an exam they couldn't pass" but added that Dublin was fairly satisfied this was not London's game plan. Sinn Féin sources also assumed the British stance would soften: some believed it already had, in fact, until Sir Patrick Mayhew recently reiterated the precise formula he had laid down in the springtime, stipulating that some arms had to be handed over.

In recent months at least some in Dublin thought London was seeking Irish help to get itself off the de-commissioning hook on which it was impaled. Only at this late stage is it emerging that the British regard it not as a hook but, apparently, as a bedrock position.

The British attitude has been partly fashioned from the convictions of ministers, and partly because the government believes it should be reflecting Unionist concerns. There can be no round-table talks before de-commissioning starts, ministers argue, because Unionists simply would not go to them and this would retard rather than advance the peace process.

The fundamental point of difference between the governments lies in their view of how to treat Gerry Adams. London is for testing his commitment to peace; Dublin has no doubt of it. London want to push him; Dublin view him as the man who delivered the ceasefire, and believes he should be not pressurised but rather helped in his on-going debates with sceptics inside his movement.

Mr Adams has repeatedly spoken of a crisis in the peace process and continually demands all-party talks. Until the de-commissioning issue is cleared up, in some ingenious way which has not yet been aired, such talks are impossible. The question then arises of whether the Adams ceasefire policy can withstand pressures inside his movement from those who argue that Britain is more concerned with disarming the IRA than doing serious business with Sinn Féin.

The two governments worked closely on many matters, but the de-commissioning question continued to expose a deep difference of opinion.

7 SEPTEMBER 1995   THE INDEPENDENT

Washington 3: the condition too far

At the heart of the disagreement between London and Dublin is what is coming to be known as "Washington 3" – the last of three conditions laid down by Sir Patrick Mayhew in a speech in Washington on 7 March.

⌐Sir Patrick said that republicans would firstly have to demonstrate a willingness in principle to disarm, and secondly come to an understanding on the practicalities of de-commissioning. Then, in Washington 3, he insisted on "the actual de-commissioning of some arms" in advance of round-table talks.⌐

In the opinion of many observers that one small phrase has the capacity to derail the entire peace process, for the Anglo-Irish disagreement over it is a symptom of a vast gulf in perception that exists between Britain and Ireland.

To conservative middle England it may seem common sense to assume that, if the IRA is genuine in indicating that it has abandoned terrorism, the organisation should now methodically set about the task of divesting itself of its sizeable armoury.

To much of nationalist Ireland, however, insistence on an arms handover is actually a more dangerous step than allowing the guns to stay out there. This is because of the fear that any present attempt to de-commission would lead to a split in the republican movement and hence a resumption of violence.

After the Washington speech Dublin signalled its strong belief that it did not believe this should be a precondition for talks, since in its opinion Gerry Adams could not deliver any arms. Sir Patrick Mayhew, by contrast, seems to believe that Mr Adams could deliver but has simply chosen not to.

Dublin's nightmare scenario, and the reason it called off the summit, was that it would be drawn into endorsing a British position which it regards as profoundly mistaken. It believes that sticking to Washington 3, far from delivering arms, is a recipe for protracted stalemate; and that in a permanent stand-off the ceasefire, and the peace process, would gradually unravel.

In the run-up to the summit the British would not move from Washington 3 and the Irish would not move towards it. In these circumstances the Irish saw no point in proceeding with the proposed disarming commission, since it viewed the commission as essentially a device to get everyone off their hooks.

The British view is that the strength of the Adams leadership is robust enough to endure a fair amount of pressure; that it must be confronted with Washington 3 until it moves; and that this is the way to advance the process. The Dublin view is that Mr Adams has stuck his neck out far enough in bringing about the ceasefire; that if he stuck if out further it might be chopped off; and that pushing Washington 3 could test the whole process to the point of destruction.

To British observers it may seem unacceptable to think of Sinn Féin making its way to the conference table without a single IRA bullet being produced, but to nationalist Ireland things look different, since there is a long tradition of allowing the guns to fall into disuse rather than insisting they be surrendered.

The British may be affronted by the idea of people sitting at the negotiating table while their friends remain armed; the Irish tend to point out that it has always been done that way, and indeed is still being done that way in places like Bosnia and the Middle East.

Republicans can also point out that they are not the only armed element in Northern Ireland: there are many loyalists with guns, and indeed more than one Unionist politician has a shady past. In the Irish Republic the fact that more than one of its mainstream parties was founded by one-time gunmen provides historical sanction for simply leaving the guns to rust.

The question of the state of opinion within the notoriously secretive republican movement is a difficult one, and it has to be said that Dublin has a better record than London in divining what is going on in those murky waters.

The previous Dublin government took huge political risks, far greater than any taken by John Major, in pursuing the peace process while IRA and loyalist killings still continued. This was based on a sense that the republican leadership was genuine.

The entire British intelligence apparatus, on the other hand, failed to predict the IRA's complete cessation of violence: security chiefs readily admit they were expecting perhaps a three-month ceasefire. It is this same intelligence apparatus which is apparently assuring government ministers that Mr Adams has room for manoeuvre, and that the way ahead is to keep pushing for Washington 3.

Meanwhile, important events were taking place within Unionism. James Molyneaux stepped down after 16 years as Ulster Unionist party leader, maintaining his low profile to the last: he sent out a short fax which said that, having reached his 75th birthday, he had decided to resign. The fax concluded with characteristic Molyneaux dryness: "Might I make it absolutely clear that I have no intention of making further comment on my decision."
For Unionism it was the end of an era.

Molyneaux swept aside by the tide of change

James Molyneaux may today be reflecting on his old friend and mentor Enoch Powell's bleak observation that all political careers end in failure. He will himself judge his long career on one point above all others: the state of the union between Northern Ireland and Britain. His judgement on the condition of that union, and its prospects, is unlikely to give him great cheer.

His quarter-century in the Commons was dedicated to strengthening the union, cementing British sovereignty over Northern Ireland and keeping the Irish Republic at bay. Yet the union today has changed dramatically, and not in the way he favours.

When he entered parliament in 1970 Unionists routinely described Northern Ireland as an integral part of the United Kingdom. The union is still there, but it has taken on a distinctly green tinge and has been viewed by successive British governments through an Anglo-Irish prism.

As leader of the largest party in Northern Ireland, Mr Molyneaux might have been expected to be at the centre of political activity. Yet for a decade and a half he steadily evaded not only the publicity limelight but also many forms of political activity. Uninterested in talks and negotiations, he regularly decried summitry and inter-party talks and condemned political initiatives. This was because he believed, with Mr Powell, that the focal point of politics should be at Westminster rather than Belfast.

He believed in the integration of Northern Ireland and Britain, hoping to help bring this about by changes in obscure parliamentary procedure. While others were immersed in momentous developments such as the 1985 Anglo-Irish agreement and the ceasefires, Mr Molyneaux concentrated on matters such as Orders in Council and select committees.

He failed to convince even a majority of his own party that such arcane matters were the real stuff of politics but, since no one else within Unionism offered a more promising alternative approach, he remained as leader for 16 years. Within his own party most regard his integrationism as an idea whose time has gone.

139

Despite his advanced years Mr Molyneaux would probably have wished to continue as party leader, but a series of errors over the past year made his departure inevitable. He went along with the Downing Street declaration because he did not believe that the IRA would halt its campaign.

He thought he had a hold on John Major because of the Prime Minister's wish to secure Unionist support in the Commons lobbies, but this illusion of influence was cruelly shattered when Mr Major produced a blueprint for the future, the framework document, which proposed ever-closer links with the Republic. Then the party threw away the North Down by-election which it could have won with a better-known candidate and a better-organised campaign.

To his eternal credit, Mr Molyneaux always sternly opposed any contemplation of the use of violence, a temptation which not all loyalist politicians have resisted. But, in common with other Unionist leaders, he failed to generate a Big Idea which could get Unionism off the defensive, give it a wider appeal, and provide it with a new vision.

The new leader of the Ulster Unionist party was to be chosen by the party grassroots, the 800-plus people who made up the Ulster Unionist Council. The council decided on a historic venue to make its choice.

8 SEPTEMBER 1995   THE INDEPENDENT

Historic citadel where Unionists will decide

The Ulster Hall, where the Ulster Unionist party is to choose its new leader, has for more than a century played a pivotal role in the political, religious and cultural life of the city of Belfast.

It has played host to notables as diverse as King George V, Lord Randolph Churchill, the Rev Ian Paisley, various wrestlers and, earlier this year, Martha and the Vandellas. It has particular historical links with the Churchill family.

Above all, it is associated with the beginnings of the Ulster Unionist movement and the foundation of the Northern Ireland state itself. With Northern Ireland possibly on the brink of a once-in-a-generation opportunity for peace, this meeting could itself prove to be a historic moment.

The hall, which sits in Belfast city centre, has an undistinguished exterior, described by the acerbic architectural commentator Charles Brett as "rather lumpish and elephantine". He adds: "It was originally crowned by a rather pleasant coat of arms, but in 1959 the loyal burgesses of Belfast rendered themselves ridiculous by removing this and replacing it with a crude concrete red hand, from which the paint is continually peeling."

It was here in 1886 that Lord Randolph Churchill, who famously declared, "Ulster will fight and Ulster will be right", urged thousands of Protestants to resist Home Rule. He was given a rapturous reception as he concluded: "Wave Ulster, all thy banners wave, and charge with all thy chivalry."

A quarter of a century later Lord Randolph's son Winston, then First Lord of the Admiralty, was invited to speak in the same hall. But in one of the great ironies of the history of Unionism, Winston was at that point, in 1912, a Liberal and a supporter of Home Rule.

A crisis developed as Unionists, outraged by the idea of a Churchill using the hallowed Ulster Hall to advocate Home Rule, said they would prevent the meeting taking place. After some days of standoff Churchill announced that he was switching venues, telling Unionists with heavy sarcasm: "There will thus be no necessity for your friends to endure the hardships of a vigil or sustain the anxieties of a siege. Neither will it be necessary for you to break the law in an attempt to deprive us forcibly of the use of property to which we are law-fully entitled." He did come to Belfast, but spoke instead in a nationalist area near the Falls Road. He was cheered by Catholics but loyalists booed and jeered him, threw rotten fish and almost overturned his motor car.

In 1912 the Ulster Hall was one of the venues used by Edward Carson, James Craig and other Unionist leaders to express their readiness to use force to resist Home Rule. At a huge rally there Carson was presented with a silk banner said to have been carried before King William III at the Battle of the Boyne.

The following day, 28 September, the leaders gathered in the hall for a religious service. Then, escorted by a guard of honour, they walked to the city hall to become the first of the 471,000 loyalists who signed a solemn covenant pledging themselves to oppose Home Rule by "all means which may be found necessary".

Thereafter the Ulster Hall became something of a citadel of Unionism, whose honour had to be defended. When three Labour candidates booked the hall in 1921 Protestants barricaded it against them and proclaimed in a telegram: "Mass meeting of loyal shipyard workers have captured Ulster Hall from Bolsheviks."

As the years passed it was used for dances, concerts and boxing and wrestling matches. In the 1960s the Rolling Stones performed there: so did the Rev Ian Paisley, who used it for many of his early rallies.

More than 800 Unionist delegates will gather in the same hall where their forefathers successfully defied the British government 83 years ago. That was a defining moment for Unionism: this election could well be another one.

A journey to Fermanagh, to test the mood in the grassroots, gave an insight into Unionist thinking.

8 SEPTEMBER 1995   THE INDEPENDENT

The Kerr family: Unionism traditional and modern

"Aye," said a man who knows Bertie Kerr. "He'd be a good Unionist to talk to, you'll meet no more decent man in a long day's walk. He'd be typical enough. His son isn't afraid to speak up either." And so it proved.

The Kerrs are a pleasant family who live in a lovely place, a spotlessly tidy farmhouse with a commanding view over a beautiful part of Fermanagh, Northern Ireland's lakeland. Eighty miles from Belfast, 14 from the border, a place of unspoilt rolling green countryside, of loughs and trout lakes, of scenery of understated beauty. But a nearby slightly dilapidated Orange hall, Union Jack fluttering outside, serves as a reminder that it is also a land of perpetually unfinished political business.

Bertie Kerr is one of more than 800 delegates who are to gather in Belfast's

Two generations of Unionism: Councillor Bertie Kerr and his son David on their Fermanagh farm

Ulster Hall to choose the next leader of the Ulster Unionists. Their decision may well be a historic one, indicating whether Unionism is to participate in the peace process or remain on the sceptical sidelines.

The Kerrs are a most welcoming family. Mrs Kerr settled us in the living room, with its quietly spectacular views, providing tea, scones, butter and jam. Bertie

143

arrived in from the farm in his working clothes, having tended to his beef cattle and pedigree Charollais.

His son David appeared in jeans and check shirt, a tall intense young man, and he and his father sat on either side of the Aga range. Bertie is friendly but has no airs and graces: indeed like many Protestants this is a matter of some pride with him. He referred to it as soon as he was asked what sort of direction the party should take.

"In my opinion it's very simple," he began in his mellifluous Fermanagh accent. "We've been our straight, honest, blunt selves for the last 25 years and we've took a hell of a battering and we've stayed together and we still have our pride and we still have our authority and our majority. And I think it's a bad time to be changing tack, quite honestly."

Bertie Kerr is a councillor and a member of the party executive, but when it comes to the vote he and the rest of the delegates will all be equal, the party hierarchy and the grassroots casting just one vote each. Some of the 800-plus have a close involvement in politics but others have only an occasional interest, which makes voting patterns difficult to predict.

London leader writers may be urging the delegates to branch out and opt for radical new directions, but the heart of the party consists of men and women like Bertie: wary, conservative people who show few signs of aching for intoxicating new departures.

The slate of five MPs – Ken Maginnis, William Ross, the Rev Martin Smyth, John Taylor and David Trimble – spans a spectrum from the immovable to those who might be innovators. But it is heavily loaded towards the former, and Bertie reflects the party's inclination towards caution.

He goes on: "We've held it together and we've kept it together. Having held the fort for 25 years, and after 25 years of burying our dead, I certainly don't want to do anything very sudden or very outrageous to the Unionist party at the present time.

"We have to be damn careful and we have to play our cards very close to our chest. We're very much on our own: we've Irish-Americans against us, the SDLP, Irish republicans, the southern government, the British government – and they all have the one aim, and that's to get over this Unionist problem. We stand very much on our own, and we need a man that's not easy pulled about."

As he spoke his son sat listening intently, sipping his tea. David, who is 21, has just started work as a trainee solicitor in Enniskillen after three years studying law in Manchester. He would like to get into Unionist politics but, unlike his father, he thinks the time has come for innovation.

"I got my eyes opened when I went to England," he says. "I got away from the Fermanagh Protestant environment, away from the flag-waving and all. And

144

you go away and you're in an impartial environment, mixing with people of all different cultures, and you look back and you say, 'What the hell's wrong with us, where are we going wrong?'

"Everybody across the water just sees it as an Orange and Green issue, but it doesn't have to be that way. It can be argued out in real terms, and that's the way I want to see our politics go. It's because of the sectarianism, because of the propaganda and the rhetoric and the grip the churches and the politicians have over the people. I'd like to sweep all that aside."

David Kerr argues for a new Unionism which would go beyond the Protestant community – all 800 people in the Ulster Hall can be expected to be Protestants – and look attractive both to Catholics and to people in Britain.

"I believe now we have a new opportunity," he says. "We're entering a new era. If we can hold on to the ceasefire and stabilise the country I think Unionism can change and can become a broader political ideal. It can become more acceptable to more people. I keep coming back to this when I'm talking to Da about how Unionism should go forward. I believe we should be trying to sell it politically, economically, socially and culturally. We have to focus on increasing our electorate and marginalising militancy. We need a leader who can do that – a leader who is good with the media, who is good with convincing both Unionists and nationalists and people across the water."

The Bertie Kerr listening to his son's youthful idealism has been fashioned by centuries of history. At least seven generations have lived in frontier Fermanagh, around Derrygonnelly, Garrison and Ballinamallard, for 250 years. He served six years in the RAF, six or seven in the B Specials, seven years in the Ulster Defence Regiment.

More than 30 friends and security force colleagues have been killed by the IRA. One night in the 1970s he didn't go out with his usual UDR patrol because he was tired. The patrol stopped to check out a parked car less than a mile from the Kerr farmhouse: it blew up, killing Alfie Johnston and Bertie's best mate, Jimmy Eames.

Bertie says the IRA tried to kill him at least once, but adds he has a lot of Catholic friends – "that may have kept me reasonably safe because I wouldn't have been a popular man to kill," he says with a smile. But, as a councillor, would Catholics vote for him?

"Well, they've not yet come round to voting for a Unionist councillor, except for a handful of people, but they have this thing that if you don't push them into a corner they'll not lift their coat and go out and vote against you; they don't go out at all. In some Orange circles and right-wing Unionist circles they give the Catholic community no credit at all, but I know very well that there are good decent people in the Catholic tradition in Fermanagh."

So what about his son's proposition that they might be brought to actually

145

support the Unionist party? "Now, they're not going to fall over themselves to vote Unionist. In one way David's absolutely correct; but the thing that worries me is that if you change tack and open your party up to this, that and the other you can lose some of your traditional support."

David interrupts him to say with some animation that the party need not change anything substantial about Unionism and did not have to lose its traditional support. "All I'm saying is that we have to shake off this sectarian sort of cloak, this Orange cloak that smothers Unionism. It's been strangling it for far too long, and it's going to sink the ship."

"Your traditional support is not going to be easy brought with you," his father replies. "You know it's going to take a bit of time to convince those people. We're at such a critical stage of negotiation, and there's so many pressures on us, that we're not in a position to take severe risks. If we could get an agreement that would be a different matter, but at the moment I wouldn't be for taking risks."

David says: "The party needs young blood. I've been at Unionist meetings with Da, and I've seen graphically how backward their thought processes are. I think there's a real lack of vision there; I think they're still living in the past."

"I know Irish republicans seem to be having more success than us," says Bertie, "but it would be a very poor, very bad move on behalf of the Unionist party to start changing now. Maybe the new man would be more amenable to the media than James Molyneaux was, but he was a good leader. I'd like to see a man who would lead the party on much a similar line."

David says: "I don't believe you should be reliant on a head count of Orangemen, on a head count of Protestants and just say, 'Well, we have those people, those people are going to vote for us, Unionism is secure as long as we have those numbers.' We have to build trust between the people, and I believe one of the ways forward is through integrated education."

Bertie shakes his head: "I wouldn't agree with that, now." But he concedes: "OK, we do need changes, but we need a bit of progress and a bit of power before we start to implement them." Electing the new leader, he says, would be the most important thing he will do this year, because the party is the main bulwark for their British citizenship and their Protestant Unionist culture against Irish republicanism.

And then his deepest fear comes to the surface. "If we get taken over and the Irish Mafia get their way, they'd be putting the foot down very hard on our culture and everything to do with us, and we haven't any place to go." At that point it becomes clear that this election goes far, far beyond mere politics.

In the view of Bertie and most of those who will be marking their ballot papers, this is not just about winning or losing elections. It is about culture, heritage, a question of survival. To the outsider those green Fermanagh hills are beautiful: to Bertie they are something which must be guarded with eternal vigilance against that feared Irish foot.

The Ulster Hall meeting produced a surprise result. Almost everyone thought the new leader would be Strangford MP John Taylor, but delegates instead voted in the youngest – and most militant – of the five candidates, David Trimble.

11 SEPTEMBER 1995   THE INDEPENDENT

Trimble wins: will peace lose?

M ost non-Unionist politicians and observers throughout Ireland have spent the weekend in undisguised dismay as they contemplate the election of David Trimble as leader of the Ulster Unionist party. Of several dozen people privately offering their opinions of the new leader, almost all regarded his elevation as disastrous for the party, the peace process and community relations generally. The universality of the gloom is striking.

Non-Unionist opinion had a benign scenario all worked out. The victor, everyone thought, was to be John Taylor, a tough old campaigner who, though hardline, would nonetheless have the clout and the vision to take his people, eventually, into the peace process and hence into a new era of accommodation between Unionists and nationalists, Britain and Ireland.

Instead they got David Trimble, who in a quarter of a century has built a reputation as an ill-tempered, unalloyed hardliner. Northern Ireland's largest

The new face of Ulster Unionism: David Trimble succeeds James Molyneaux as leader of Northern Ireland's largest political party

political grouping has just elected a figure whom most non-Unionists regard with something close to horror.

"He has the shortest fuse in Irish politics," said one observer. Another noted: "He gets more angry more quickly than anyone else I know." There was much recent astonishment when an editorial in *The Times* referred to him as a moderate. "I was having my breakfast when I read that," a government minister said. "Nearly puked up my Frosties."

The fact is that the party opted for the most militant hardliner of the five candidates on offer, and elected him by a handsome margin. Furthermore, he appears to have been given the job largely because of his tough and uncompromising line, particularly at "the siege of Drumcree" in July.

This was the incident, now reverentially commemorated by an Orange medal which has just been awarded to the new leader, in which he played a leading role in pressurising police to allow an Orange march through a Catholic district in his Upper Bann constituency. Although the episode was condemned as a community relations disaster, his party approved of it so much that it probably swung the contest for him.

He has a long history of association with extreme positions. For many years a law lecturer at Queen's University Belfast, he entered politics in the early 1970s with Vanguard. This was a movement set up because its members believed the Unionist party was too soft and compromising.

Vanguard was both a political party fighting elections and an umbrella group for an assembly of loyalist organisations, some of them paramilitary groups. Its leader, William Craig MP, a former Stormont cabinet minister who underwent a Mosley-style conversion to mass action, organised a series of monster rallies in which he inspected thousands of men drawn up in ranks. He was widely condemned for what became known as "shoot-to-kill" speeches in which he openly threatened the use of force.

Paradoxically, Mr Craig later not only converted back to conventional politics but unexpectedly produced a scheme for "voluntary coalition" which would allow Catholics into a new Stormont cabinet. Other Unionist leaders, in particular the Rev Ian Paisley, were so appalled by his new-found moderation that they ejected him – and Mr Trimble, a faithful follower – from the Unionist mainstream.

Vanguard split, Mr Craig becoming leader of a small rump with Mr Trimble as his deputy. This is regarded as Mr Trimble's only serious foray into moderation. When their movement fell apart in the late 1970s both men quietly rejoined the main Unionist party. But the party, it was plain, did not quickly take Mr Trimble to its heart, and it took him many years to work his way back into the mainstream.

When the Anglo-Irish agreement arrived in 1985 he stayed in the party but also joined the Ulster Clubs, a new organisation dedicated to using more militant methods to bring down the accord. Ulster Clubs leader Alan Wright frequently used violent rhetoric, declaring: "Faced with treachery as we are today, I cannot see anything other than the Ulster people on the streets prepared to use legitimate force."

Mr Trimble said at this time that he had no objection in principle to "mobilisation and citizens' army calls", adding: "I would personally draw the line at terrorism and serious violence. But if we are talking about a campaign that involves demonstrations and so on, then a certain element of violence may be inescapable."

The Ulster Clubs episode – which eventually faded away in miserable failure – was a decade ago, and Vanguard was two decades ago, but memories are

149

long in Ireland. The lasting significance of these two important phases in his career is their relevance to the IRA arms de-commissioning debate.

The new Unionist leader's position is that republicans should not be admitted fully to the democratic processes until their commitment to exclusively peaceful methods is established. His opponents can hardly be expected to refrain from recalling his membership of two organisations whose leaders spoke publicly about the use of force.

His political career finally took off in 1990 when he won the by-election caused by the death of Harold McCusker. Since then his rise has been, by Unionism's generally glacial standards, positively meteoric. In particular he has emerged as one of Unionism's most effective media performers – a highly important factor in a party whose last leader, James Molyneaux, was in television terms practically invisible. If he has also displayed excitability and a tendency to become red, flushed and angry, this clearly did not deter delegates from voting for him.

They were aware they were choosing a leader who has shown no serious signs of attempting any outreach to Catholics and nationalists, and whose personal attitude towards Catholics, and the British and Irish governments, is marked by deep suspicion.

Optimists will point out that De Klerk did not look like a De Klerk before he became president of South Africa, and that as leader Mr Trimble will have to confront the reality of the peace process and come to terms with it. Perhaps so: but it has to be said that this is the leader whom nobody outside Unionism wanted; that he has come to power on a very hardline ticket; and that 25 years in politics have left no real indication that he has a vision beyond Unionism and Orangeism.

Although the state of opinion in the republican camp often gave cause for concern, on the loyalist side the ceasefire never seriously looked like breaking down.

October 1995 brought the first anniversary of the loyalist cessation. Billy Hutchinson, the ex-prisoner who a year earlier had clashed with Iris Robinson of the DUP (*see* "Ulstermen march to a new drum", pp. 38–41), had become a leading light in the Progressive Unionist party. During the course of the year he had the experience of meeting government ministers and officials more than a dozen times. He had become a confident and self-assured political performer, with a message that, on the loyalist side at least, the peace was solid.

13 OCTOBER 1995   THE INDEPENDENT

Shankill takes to the peace process

Twenty years ago Billy Hutchinson, as a young Shankill Road loyalist, believed the best way to deal with republicanism was through violence. He was part of an Ulster Volunteer Force gang which shot two men dead on the Falls Road, an action which put him behind bars for 15 years. His view of how to deal with republicans has changed dramatically. "One of the things that would worry me is if people try to screw Sinn Féin," he says now. "I don't think anybody should be trying to do that, I don't think there's anything in it for anybody to screw them."

In place of the old belligerence, and indeed the ferocity for which the loyalist paramilitary groups were known, there is now, according to Mr Hutchinson, a new political way of looking at things. "We need to convince Sinn Féin that there is a democratic process and that they can have a role in it as a democratic party. I think we should assist them in every way to come into it fully," he says.

Mr Hutchinson, an intense man of 39, describes the Progressive Unionist party as political confidants of the illegal Ulster Volunteer Force. The PUP and the

Ulster Democratic party, which speaks for the illegal Ulster Defence Association, have made a considerable impact since the loyalist ceasefire, surprising and heartening many that such moderate messages should come from such an unexpected quarter.

The past year has seen many contacts with government, with Mr Hutchinson leading PUP delegations on 15 occasions to meet senior civil servants and ministers. One of the main points in these discussions has been the de-commissioning of paramilitary weaponry, the issue on which the government and Sinn Féin have been deadlocked for many months. The loyalist view, as set out by Billy Hutchinson, is actually not far from that of the republicans.

He says: "For me it's whether the guns are being used or not being used that is the most important thing. If people can guarantee that they're not going to be used then I wouldn't be very concerned. If the Sinn Féin position is that it should never happen then I think there's something wrong with that. But I don't think de-commissioning should be a precondition for talks. In our discussions with the government we talked about the ways in which weapons could be de-commissioned. For example, there could be some sort of agreement that people transporting guns would not be arrested. We talked about whether people would drive them to police stations, or dig up caches then leave them at a certain place and inform the police. We talked about whether the people that handed them over might be forensically connected to the guns. Those were the sort of things that were thrown up for discussion, but no answers were ever given."

Mr Hutchinson believes it has been a good year for his movement, though he is disappointed that all-party talks have not been convened, that prisoners have not been released and that more trust has not been built up. He is, however, convinced that the leaders of loyalist paramilitarism have no intention of going back to war: "One thing I'm confident of is that the loyalists are united and 100 per cent behind the peace. Now I wouldn't say there is not an appetite for war among some individuals – it would be wrong to say everybody's on board for peace.

"But those people will abide by what the leadership says. The analysis we gave over a year ago was the correct one, that there was no sellout. The acid test will come when we actually move into all-party talks and we start talking about settlements. I think that's when people will start to get jittery, whenever the questions start coming up about organisations being disbanded and so on. But that's way down the road."

In the meantime he is involved not just in a peace process but in a learning process. The past year has seen him and his colleagues meeting dozens of people from all over the world, ranging from American Senators to South African academics. He says: "We're still learning how to put ourselves in someone else's

152

shoes and see it from their point of view, whether they're the British government or Sinn Féin.

"I've been particularly surprised how the mainstream Unionist politicians have reacted to us – they treat us as non-people, they don't understand where we, or indeed the republicans, are coming from. When David Trimble was elected [leader of the Ulster Unionist party] my first reaction was shock-horror, but in fact, like us, he's meeting a wide range of people and up to now he hasn't put a foot wrong."

And so to the key question: how strong is the peace? "It's as strong as the republicans and loyalists want it to be. I believe there is a feeling within the republican and loyalist leaderships that they don't want to put their people through any more of the trauma of the last 25 years. The worrying thing for me is that both are ready for war and for peace. At the moment we're all in peace mode but we shouldn't be under any illusions – people can go back to war whenever they want, they've got the capabilities.

"I want to make sure that they don't. We're still waiting for the peace process and the political process to merge together, and for real talks to start. Once that happens then I think we're on our way. But we need to sit down and thrash out an agreement with all the parties and with those who represent the people who carried out the violence for the last 25 years. That's the only time that the peace will be signed, sealed and delivered."

In the dispute between the government and Sinn Féin over the de-commissioning of paramilitary weaponry, it is often overlooked that the IRA are not the only illegal organisation with stockpiles of guns. The extreme Protestant groups have hundreds of guns which they used, in the two years before the ceasefires, to kill more people than did the IRA. One reason why the loyalist guns are rarely highlighted is that they have, as Billy Hutchinson illustrates, embraced the peace process with such unexpected and evidently genuine enthusiasm.

After years of relying on the gun, the loyalists have developed a curious empathy with the republicans: they know where they are coming from, they know how difficult it is to make peace, and they know the heavy price which all would pay in going back to war. The striking difference between the loyalists and the republicans is the apparent lack of strains and pressures within the extreme Protestant underworld. Within Sinn Féin and the IRA there are signs that many of the grassroots are frustrated and dissatisfied with the pace and direction of the peace process. On the loyalist side, however, there is no real sign of any pressure for a return to war. That is not to say that paramilitarism is dwindling: the UVF and UDA are still out there, carrying out punishment beatings and showing no sign of de-commissioning their weapons.

The transformation of what was the most militant part of loyalism into an element hungry for negotiation and prepared to compromise is only part of the wider Unionist scene. The election of David Trimble as Ulster Unionist party leader shows that some sections of Protestant opinion are moving towards a tougher line. It seems unlikely that parties such as the PUP and UDP will make a spectacular electoral dent in Mr Trimble's party. Old voting habits are notoriously difficult to change in Northern Ireland, and many Unionists will consider the new parties too working-class, too left-leaning and too close to the paramilitants. They are therefore probably destined to remain as fringe parties.

But the fact that the loyalist paramilitaries have embraced politics with such relish is already having a significant effect. In the past many Unionist politicians were able to point over their shoulders at the violent Protestant groups and cite them as evidence of how hardline their grassroots were. Old patterns are changing: the paramilitary groups are no longer willing to provide the muscle for politicians to use. This means the politicians will be compelled to rely less on threats and more on straightforward politics. The fact that they will henceforth have to depend on force of argument, rather than the argument of force, is changing the face of Unionist politics.

The autumn of 1995 brought a stream of ominous noises from Gerry Adams and other republican leaders, warning that the British attitude on de-commissioning was endangering the peace process.

The planned Anglo-Irish summit eventually took place late in November after intense negotiations. Although these failed to break the deadlock, the setting up of an international body to report on the de-commissioning issue seemed to edge the process forward.

Creative fudge that may ease the log jam

The late-night Anglo-Irish summit and subsequent communiqué may go down in diplomatic history as an object lesson in how to make a fair number of bricks when faced with a distinct lack of straw.

The two governments were at an impasse on the crucial question of de-commissioning. London said some arms must be de-commissioned; Dublin feared this precondition could test Gerry Adams and the republican movement to the point of destruction. A summit scheduled for September had been postponed at the last moment amid some acrimony, and ever since then neither side showed any sign of budging. As time went by, without an agreement and without the prospect of early talks, there were more and more reports that the IRA might abandon the peace process and return to terrorism.

The communiqué has been dismissed as a fudge, but there is a case to be made that it was a most ingenious and creative means of facing up to the basic disagreement and making the most of it. Some aspects of it are hard for Sinn Féin to swallow, but there is enough in it to make a resort to violence in the immediate future all but inconceivable.

It is difficult to judge just how real was the risk of a return to violence. Irritation, frustration and anger are certainly evident in the republican camp, but this did not mean a return to violence was inevitable. Republican strategists are keenly aware that even one bomb would destroy all the relationships they have painstakingly built up with important political elements in Ireland and America.

The fact is that Sinn Féin have little choice but to accept the communiqué as the basis for the next phase of the peace process. They are not in a position to stay out of talks, even if these will only be talks about talks; and they are not in a position to boycott an international body on arms de-commissioning, especially since it will be chaired by such a senior American political figure as former senator George Mitchell.

Furthermore, the preparatory talks about talks give the appearance of being a serious exercise rather than the type of desultory encounters seen often in the

155

past. With the commission, meanwhile, they will be able to raise any matters they wish. They can therefore be expected to make the case that security-force weapons should be taken into account, as well as illegally held guns, and to argue forcibly that the British government's stand on de-commissioning is unreasonable. Of critical importance to the republicans is the fact that the Taoiseach, John Bruton, did not break with them on the de-commissioning issue and endorse the British position. Sinn Féin had been worried that he might abandon them in favour of strengthening his relations with Mr Major and the Unionists, but this did not happen.

On the Unionist side the communiqué will pose a dilemma for Unionist party leader David Trimble. He has had a well-received honeymoon period, winning widespread approval of his willingness to meet a wide range of political leaders, including Mr Bruton. The communiqué contains a nod in his direction by including his suggestion that an elected body could play a part in negotiations. He now faces the choice of proceeding on the basis of the communiqué, thus extending his honeymoon period, or of a retreat back to the unpopular laager. That laager is already occupied by the Rev Ian Paisley's Democratic Unionist party, which has pledged itself not to take part in talks while the IRA remains in existence. The other players accept that the DUP will not be at the table, at least in the first instance.

The achievement of the communiqué is to apply such pressures, on both republicans and Unionists, even though the two governments are not in agreement. The weakness, however, is that it has not resolved the de-commissioning issue: that still lies ahead, and still retains the capacity to derail the entire process.

In the meantime, however, it has established a breathing space. One Dublin source said: "It hasn't resolved any problems, just given space which might be used to get people off hooks." Dublin still aims to help London off the de-commissioning hook: the problem is that London seems to regard it not as a hook but as a fundamental principle. Perhaps the most significant point in the communiqué may yet turn out to be the largely overlooked sentence which says that preparatory talks could cover the de-commissioning issue. This in effect throws the issue open for all parties to make an input – something which could either solidify the log jam or loosen it.

When US President Bill Clinton first intervened in Northern Ireland matters, in January 1994, he did so in a most

controversial way, by granting Gerry
Adams a visa to visit America despite
intense British opposition.

In the following months, however, his
administration made efforts to repair its
relations with Britain and to reach out to
Unionist opinion. The success of those
efforts was illustrated when Clinton visited
Northern Ireland and received a
rapturous reception.

A formula for reviving
Irish spirits

Belfast, as somebody once remarked, is not at all a typical Irish city: it has more in common with the Scottish or northern English cities which sprang up with the industrial revolution, and shares many of their characteristics.

In one of its aspects it is tough, dour, grumpy, with a take-it-or-leave-it attitude, a city of no airs and graces – personified, in fact, by Van Morrison, who served as the warm-up act for Bill Clinton at its city hall. That facet has been to the fore ever since the paramilitary ceasefires of 1994, which were greeted with a mixture of relief and caution. It took the presidential visit to liberate another of the city's aspects, at last allowing it to show its warm, welcoming, even joyous, face.

In doing so, the visit not only provided the occasion for a release of good will but also consolidated and cemented the peace process. It was more than just a great party: it may turn out to be a truly historic turning point, for in a single day almost all of the lingering doubts about the peace were swept away.

Many trials and obstacles will have to be surmounted in the months and years ahead, but these events have immeasurably strengthened the process. The

157

President Bill Clinton responding to the cheers and applause at Belfast City Hall

preceding weeks had produced a series of ever-gloomier assessments from republicans, and latterly from security sources. Both elements warned that the process was becoming unstable as the arms de-commissioning impasse dragged on.

The late-night Anglo-Irish summit, since overshadowed by the Clinton visit, did much to relieve the pressures. Even in the absence of agreement between Dublin and London, its carefully balanced formula set up an international body on de-commissioning and moved towards talks. It was in effect an offer which, politically, Sinn Féin and the IRA could not refuse, and, for the moment at least, it dispelled most of the dangerous tensions.

While the ingenious intricacies of the summit communiqué have supplied a technical framework for the next few months, the Clinton visit delivered an extraordinary injection of momentum, enthusiasm, fresh heart and new spirit. His message that the violence was over for good was radiated back to him from the thousands who stood in the cold to hear him and cheer him.

On 31 August, on the first anniversary of the IRA cessation of violence, the streets in front of the city hall were empty: no one felt able to celebrate. With Clinton as the catalyst, tens of thousands clapped, cheered, waved their US flags and finally allowed their feelings to come out into the open. The fact that the crowd was made up of both Catholics and Protestants is a tribute to Clinton's political skills. Throughout 1994 his name was mud with Unionists as, in the face of stiff British opposition, he granted Gerry Adams visas to visit the States and allowed him to fund-raise there (a boon which has netted Sinn Féin hundreds of thousands of dollars and has probably made it Ireland's richest political party).

Clinton's is the first US administration to make a serious study of the politics of Northern Ireland, and certainly the first to intervene in them. No American president had ever visited Northern Ireland before, JFK deciding in 1963 not to venture north of the border. This was largely because American governments were perceived as pro-Irish nationalist and therefore as anti-Unionist, as indeed many saw Clinton in 1994. Since then, however, his position has evolved considerably: he has made particular efforts to mend fences with London while, as he later demonstrated in Dublin, he has remained on good terms with the Irish government. His warmest praise was reserved for SDLP leader John Hume, who clearly has a major input into American decision making. But Clinton has also made a special effort to build bridges to Unionists, offering special access to Unionist leader David Trimble and indeed establishing relations with loyalist paramilitary groups. Keeping all sides in the conflict reasonably happy is no easy task, but the tumultuous welcomes he received in Belfast and Londonderry showed he has succeeded in doing so. (His coolest reception, from the Rev Ian Paisley, is regarded as pretty much par for the Paisley course.)

Clinton's popularity was not earned by retreating into anodyne generalisations about peace. The most important messages in his speeches were that the violence must be over for good and that formerly violent prodigals should be welcomed into politics. He declared in Belfast: "You must be willing to say to those who renounce violence that they are entitled to be part of the democratic process."

In emphasising this last point, he voiced no criticism of the British government but made it clear that his hope is for the speedy construction of an inclusive settlement. In doing so he places more emphasis on the need for dialogue than London has displayed. In his approach Clinton is, of course, hopeful of netting Irish-American votes, but his analysis goes much deeper than that. He, like Dublin, believes that the best way to deal with republicans is to draw them ever-deeper into the political net. He believes his decision to allow Adams into the States was vindicated in that it helped facilitate the IRA ceasefire, and Sinn Féin sources confirm that he is right.

The appointment of his close friend and ally George Mitchell as head of the de-commissioning body is an indication that the US will remain a major player in the peace process. Many Unionists and many in Britain may have instinctive reservations about continuing US involvement, but the fact is that it is here to stay. The flags waved for Clinton, but they also waved in sheer joy, in the first real public communal celebration of the peace.

The elation of the Clinton visit did not last long. In December the IRA demonstrated, with a series of killings on the streets of Belfast, that it was still in the business of the gun.

The attacks were aimed not at the security forces but at men said to be involved in the drugs trade or other criminality. They sent the message that, far from being about to de-commission its weapons, the IRA still felt free to use them.

21 DECEMBER 1995   THE INDEPENDENT

How the guns kept drugs out of Belfast

Somebody is killing drug dealers in Belfast. Mickey "Moneybags" Mooney was the first to go, gunned down in a city centre bar in April 1995. Another fatal shooting followed in September, and this month there have been three more.

Three of the dead men, including Moneybags, were unquestionably major full-time professional drug dealers, buying and pushing drugs on a large scale. The most recent victim, who died two days ago, was not in their league,

160

though he was awaiting trial on a charge of importing a quarter of a million pounds' worth of cannabis. The fifth killing is less clear cut, for although the victim was well known to detectives investigating armed robberies, he had only a glancing connection with drugs.

Each time news comes through that a man has been shot dead, everyone holds their breath for a moment, then relaxes when it becomes clear that the incident represents no threat to the ceasefires. Once this has been established these killings fade fast from the public memory.

The fact of these three drug-related deaths within a month is, however, raising new questions about who is responsible, and whether this much-increased killing rate could lead to a slide back to full-scale violence. Although the IRA has not admitted any of the killings, most assume they are its work.

Although the police are undoubtedly pursuing the gunmen, both the RUC and government ministers are markedly evasive in answering questions about who is doing the killings. Senior spokesmen have in effect been at pains not to accuse the IRA of responsibility: politically, the name of the game seems to be to attempt to make a distinction between political violence and vigilantism.

All this is posing fundamental questions about Northern Ireland as a society, for the chilling truth is that the attitude of many sections of opinion towards the drug killings is one of public silence but private applause. Drug dealers are regarded as the lowest of the low, and few shed tears when they meet sudden premature deaths. Such attitudes are not confined to Northern Ireland, as Michael Winner's vigilante films suggest, but there are particular reasons why Belfast does not mourn the passing of such men. For one thing, a quarter-century of terrorism has inevitably inured many to the idea of violent death.

There is another reason. Belfast may have suffered terribly from terrorism, but the Troubles had the effect of ensuring that it remained the most drugs-free city in these islands. People want it to stay that way. In the 1970s the fact that both republican and loyalist groups made it clear they would kill dealers kept the city, apart from the traditionally bohemian student districts, relatively free of drugs.

This hard-line attitude softened in the late 1980s, particularly on the loyalist side, with increasing quantities of dope and tablets gradually making their appearance. In the early 1990s the IRA maintained its puritanical anti-drugs stance but in other quarters things changed dramatically. Some minor republican groups and some major loyalist figures, seeing the profits to be made, switched from condemning the drugs trade to actively trafficking in it.

But even then there were unwritten rules and regulations. Dope and ecstasy tablets became more widely available but heroin and the like have been strictly taboo. Dublin, 100 miles and a three-hour car journey away, had thousands of heroin addicts, but in Belfast the drug was practically unknown. The IRA made its attitude clear with several large-scale operations: in 1992, in one night, it killed one drug dealer and kneecapped another ten. In 1994, a few months before its cessation of violence, scores of IRA members took part in attacks which killed one dealer and injured a further sixteen.

In the republican districts where drugs were taking hold many people openly approved of this violence against what were termed "anti-social elements", while many more displayed ambivalence. The IRA was widely regarded as keeping the problem at bay, so that when it called its ceasefire many feared it would have the unwelcome side effect of opening up Belfast to heroin and cocaine.

That was, after all, exactly what happened in South Africa in the wake of the political settlement there. Before the settlement drug abuse there was mainly confined to marijuana and pills, but since then parts of the country, including Soweto, have been flooded with cocaine as a Nigerian drug cartel set about creating a new market.

In Belfast the amount of marijuana and ecstasy tablets available rose steeply in the aftermath of the ceasefires. The RUC reinforced its drug squad, but there was widespread public concern about the possibility of a flood of drugs, including cocaine or heroin.

The shootings of the four dealers have sent a message both to local dealers and to those who might be tempted to come in from outside. After the killing of Moneybags some of his associates stood in the street outside the bar and angrily shouted: "What ceasefire? What about the ceasefire now?" The message is that the IRA cessation does not extend to the drugs trade.

The killings may well have the effect of stopping that trade from flourishing, and of keeping heroin out of Belfast. In themselves these are laudable ends: the problem is the means by which they are achieved. By targeting drugs people, the IRA projects itself as defenders of the community.

But in doing so it is keeping the flame of violence lit, demonstrating the power of the gun and projecting the pernicious message that, while political terrorism may be over, carefully directed violence is a useful tool of social control. If that continues, it will dash the hopes of those who hoped that paramilitarism would slowly but surely wither away, to be replaced eventually by a society in which the gun had no role.

The new year brought the unveiling of the report on arms de-commissioning – but within hours of publication it had been

overtaken by an unexpected
announcement in the
Commons.

25 JANUARY 1996   THE INDEPENDENT

New focus, same crisis

A ncient Greek dramas would sometimes culminate in the appearance of a *deus ex machina*, a god lowered onto the stage by means of a crane, who would use supernatural powers to sort out the muddles created by mortals. For a few hours yesterday Senator George Mitchell seemed to fit such a role. His report on arms de-commissioning seemed to have something for everyone, and while it was not clear whether Unionists could accept it, it looked likely to ease the ominous pressures within republicanism.

The senator brought to the problem a measure of American can-do pragmatism; his function was less one of divine intervention than of empirical observation, followed by practical suggestions and comment. He eased the British government off the hook of Washington 3 by simply pointing out that there was no chance of the IRA or loyalists de-commissioning weapons in advance of talks. The fact of an independent observer saying this seemed somehow to make it more acceptable, or at least tolerable.

The report's laconic effectiveness was no accident, for it was apparent both from the document itself and from his news conference that Senator Mitchell is a class act. With grace and humour he showed himself to be the most skilful political performer ever seen in Belfast since – well since the end of November, when his friend Bill Clinton was in town.

The British and Irish governments, when they set up the international body, gave it a fairly narrow remit, asking for a report on the de-commissioning issue. What they got was a report which took into account a wide spectrum of the most important issues in the peace process. The international body clearly took as its starting point not the essentially technical issue of de-commissioning but the much broader approach of working out how to advance the peace process. Concluding that no guns were in the offing, it drafted a list of six principles to which all parties to talks should subscribe. Together these represented a complete farewell to arms: if the IRA would not hand over weapons it must instead make a solemn promise to the world that the shadow of the gunman had gone.

The report created a sense of transformation – and then, within hours, John Major transformed it all over again. In what was almost a throwaway line, the report had mentioned the idea of "an elective process" – much to the relief of Mr Major, who had been banking on its appearance. The government had already done much work on the idea, and Mr Major explained to the Commons that he believed an election was the way ahead. It would, the government argued, clear the way for talks, since David Trimble had said an election would give Sinn Féin a mandate, and that he would then talk to them without the de-commissioning of weapons. This opened up the possibility of inter-party talks without an arms hand-over, a route which the government has now gratefully taken. Mr Trimble had envisaged an election to a new assembly, but in the Commons Mr Major did not use the word "assembly" and seemed to envisage a body to provide a negotiator rather than some new devolved institution. This distinction is crucial. Previous assemblies, the longest-lived of which was the Stormont parliament, are still seared into Irish nationalist folk memory as bastions of anti-Catholicism. It is no exaggeration to say that a return to anything reminiscent of this would cause large numbers of republicans to think about going back to war.

Sinn Féin had a good morning with the launch of the Mitchell document, but a bad afternoon when Mr Major introduced his election proposal. The move also angered John Hume and the Irish government, who believed Mr Major had deliberately kept them in the dark and ambushed them.

The election idea has now been elevated to the centrepiece of the peace process, where it is clearly destined to remain for many months. Even with full Labour support, it will clearly take months for the concept to be discussed, to make its way onto the statute book, and for voters to go to the polls. This means the abandonment of the existing target date for all-party talks to open at the end of February. Mr Trimble's evident pleasure at the government's action has inflamed the suspicion – never far from the surface of the nationalist psyche – that the new course was at least partly motivated by the hope of securing Unionist voting support. Whatever the truth of this, Sinn Féin find that, sixteen months on from the IRA ceasefire, the doors of the conference chamber still remain closed to them. Furthermore, they strongly suspect Mr Major of pursuing a Unionist agenda.

A day which promised a breakthrough thus ended in something close to crisis, with no easing of the long build-up of frustration within the republican movement. The Mitchell report mentioned the lack of trust in Northern Ireland: the day closed with more distrust than ever, and a sense that one crisis had been replaced by another.

164

CONCLUSION

It was a time of hope and anxiety, jubilation and doubt, optimism and nagging fears. It was the most peaceful time for a quarter of a century, but while it brought new hope it also opened up new vistas of difficulties.

The surge of relief which followed the ceasefires was palpable, but although the desire for peace was widespread it was not universal. All the centuries of paramilitarism, culminating in the 25 years of concentrated violence, left a potent tradition of readiness to resort to the gun. In the months and years ahead there are bound to be times when many will contemplate going back to it.

A new phase opened up with John Major's proposal of an election: the unanswered question is whether it could advance or retard the process. The loyalists have taken to peace with unexpected enthusiasm, and show no sign of wanting a return to war. Attention is therefore focused on the republicans.

The IRA ceasefire was a republican initiative, undertaken when the leaders of republicanism came to realise that their "armed struggle" had run its course. In return for giving it up they wanted an entry into the political processes and to inclusive talks; until they get that the peace will be a fragile one.

The republican leaders do not want to go back to war, but there will always be some in the grassroots who will have more faith in the gun. The potential breaking-point rests with the men to be seen walking around the Falls Road, the ones who have no job or who are employed only occasionally in low-paid casual work. Unemployment will continue to conspire with historical, economic and social factors to provide a pool of potential paramilitants. Many of these people feel they have no stake in society; many of them also feel that the ceasefires brought them little or no new advantage in terms of political recognition, material well-being or personal self-respect.

The year and a half since the ceasefires demonstrated that it is not easy for the Unionist community, or the British government, to think in terms of reaching out to such people. Unless this happens, however, the possibility of a new outbreak will always exist.

Those men on the Falls Road, and their fathers and grandfathers, have been politically alienated since Northern Ireland came into being. The challenge is to construct a political system big enough to encompass them and persuade them that they can have a place in society. The task of doing so will mean many difficult years ahead as all sides attempt to sustain the nervous peace.

INDEX

169

POSTSCRIPT

The conclusion of this book was written and dispatched to the printers early in February. On the evening of Friday 9 February, the IRA declared that its ceasefire was over, and an hour later detonated a huge bomb near Canary Wharf in the London Docklands. Two people were killed, dozens more were injured, destruction was widespread, and the peace process was shattered.

At the time of writing it is unclear whether the attack is an isolated incident or the prelude to a full-scale resumption of violence. There is hope that something can be salvaged from the wreckage, but there is also great fear that Northern Ireland could face a whole new cycle of the Troubles.

The following article was too late for inclusion in the book proper, but the Docklands attack was such a serious and potentially catastrophic event that we felt it should be included. The pity is that the period covered by this book should begin on a high note, with the IRA ceasefire, but end with its collapse, a moment of such dismay and fear for the future.

---

12 FEBRUARY 1996   THE INDEPENDENT

So near – yet now so far

When the bombs stopped going off in August 1994, it was understandable that many people in Britain should have concluded, with great relief, that the Troubles were over. Up close in Belfast, however, it always seemed more delicate and complicated than that.

The ceasefire was a unilateral move by the IRA, with no negotiations or discussions with the British before it was declared. The organisation was therefore free to decide on its own terms and conditions: it has never spelt these out, but they have become clear over the months. They are as follows. The IRA would remain in being, continuing to recruit and train, raise funds, and carry out surveillance on possible targets. It would carry out punishment beatings of those it considered "anti-social elements" and it reserved the right to shoot dead suspected drug dealers. It would not de-commission, destroy or hand over a single ounce of explosives, a single gun or a single bullet, since these would be acts of surrender. The IRA had called a cessation but it had disengaged, not surrendered. The republican movement had been promised entry into politics and negotiations: the IRA was waiting to see whether that promise was kept, and to give Gerry Adams a chance to try politics.

Adams had sold the ceasefire to the IRA on the basis that it would get the republican movement into serious talks with the British. His conclusion was that while the IRA had tremendous negative power through its bombs, it was not strong enough to achieve a military victory and force a British withdrawal. The argument went that the terrorist campaign had achieved a great deal and had provided the dynamic for change. The proposition was that an alternative dynamic existed in the shape of an international coalition to press the republican and nationalist cause. It was not anticipated that getting to the table would lead to a British withdrawal, but the expectation was that a strong nationalist bloc would have a powerful say. Gerry Adams would be at the table, along with John Hume and the then Taoiseach, Albert Reynolds. Also there, or thereabouts, would be Bill Clinton, as well as influential strands of Irish-American opinion. Together this bloc would win many of the arguments and would have considerable clout.

Adams was able to produce evidence that a cessation would lead to entry into such political processes. Hume had publicly stuck his neck out by issuing a series of joint statements with Adams and by proclaiming his belief that the republicans could be persuaded to turn away from violence. Clinton had shown that he accepted this by dropping the 20-year ban on Adams entering the US, and had done so despite intense British pressure. Reynolds had pushed John Major into signing the Downing Street declaration, a document which indicated that a peaceful republican movement would be allowed into talks. Hume, Reynolds and Clinton had all signalled that they were prepared to stop treating Irish republicans as pariahs, just as soon as the guns fell silent. The British were clearly more reluctant about this approach, but had nonetheless sent a strong signal in the Downing Street declaration.

This was a new type of approach to the IRA. It had become adept at fighting the army and the police: it was less sure about how to deal with offers rather than assaults. Crucially, however, Adams offered the prospect of political advance and an honourable exit from violence, the key concept being that it would be not a surrender but a historic change of direction. It took him years to formulate his proposals, and it took the IRA many months to reach the decision to announce its "complete cessation of military operations". The fact that it took so long is a telling indication that there were many doubts and opponents at various levels of the organisation. Although Sinn Féin is to most intents and purposes a public body, the IRA is an enclosed order, a profoundly militaristic group. When Sinn Féin leaders refer in private to "the army", they mean not the British army but the IRA.

The whole exercise began promisingly enough. Reynolds, Hume and Adams shook hands publicly in Dublin. Adams did several triumphant laps of honour in the States, where Clinton received him at the White House and allowed him to raise hundreds of thousands of dollars. Reynolds set up the Forum for Peace and Reconciliation, formally welcoming Sinn Féin to the political processes and bringing handshakes with every major political figure in the Republic. Adams and Martin McGuinness held rounds of exploratory talks with British officials and later with ministers. Everywhere doors which had been closed to the republicans swung open. But these, though important, were essentially warm-ups for the main event – inter-party talks – and there were also ominous signs. Reynolds fell as Taoiseach, to be replaced by the less sympathetic John Bruton. Adams kept pressing for the opening of all-party talks, but in the spring of 1995 Sir Patrick Mayhew laid out a very specific precondition: some IRA weapons would first have to be de-commissioned.

It was a full eight months after the ceasefire that Mayhew finally agreed to meet Adams, who was by that stage warning publicly of a crisis in the peace process. He quoted Seamus Heaney – "A space has been created in which hope can grow" - to indicate that republican patience was not infinite.

By August the ceasefire was showing signs of increasing strain. A source close to Adams, pressing for talks, said then: "There's a political vacuum. We need an inclusive agenda. We've had a strategy of alternative initiatives – the Dublin government, Hume, going to Washington, South Africa and so on. The trouble is, it's a year on, people aren't interested in Gerry going to Washington any more."

A Dublin source, worried that the British government was being dangerously complacent, said at that stage: "The ceasefires are a dynamic. You need a certain dynamism to hold them and they have to be underpinned by political negotiation. The fact that they are so popular doesn't necessarily mean that they are therefore irreversible. We can't rely on the threat of public anger to keep violence permanently off the screen."

The *Independent* reported: "The price of peace will be eternal vigilance – the most careful handling of all the minor dramas which might turn into a real crisis. Above all, critical judgements have continually to be made about the state of play within both republicanism and loyalism, and a watch kept for the rise of any new hawkish elements. A genuine worry for many of the other participants in the peace process is the level of competence displayed by the government. Everyone – including republicans – would be happier if London held to a more consistent line and displayed more sureness of touch in its handling of what, a year on, is a delicate process which will continue to require judicious, intricate micro-management if it is to lead to lasting peace."

It is now clear that Dublin was right to worry about the state of opinion within the republican movement, and that London made an inaccurate assessment of how much strain it would bear. In January the prior de-commissioning precondition was dropped by John Major, but it was immediately replaced by the proposal for an election. From London's point of view this may have appeared a skilful move to circumvent Unionist conditions for talks, but it also meant another considerable delay before getting to the table. Mr Major would clearly not have gone for an election had he believed it would push the IRA back to violence: obviously the intelligence analysis at his disposal was badly, tragically wrong.

This was probably the last straw for the IRA. It is not difficult to persuade republicans, raised as they are on the concept of perfidious Albion, that the British are up to their old duplicitous tricks again. Prior de-commissioning, which had been presented by London as an article of faith, was simply dropped in favour of a new precondition: republicans saw this as proof that the weapons issue was used in a blatantly tactical way, its real purpose being delay.

The election of David Trimble as leader of the Ulster Unionist party had raised Unionism's stock, but it also increased republican suspicions that Mr Major's handling of the peace process was increasingly influenced by the desire for Unionist support in the division lobbies.

Probably above all else, there was the feeling in republican circles that the British were not serious about bringing Sinn Féin in from the cold. The introduction of the election idea meant that, 17 months on from the ceasefire, the conference table was as remote as ever. To republicans the British seemed intent not on doing serious business with them but on belittling them, on resisting the demand for talks, on stringing them along, possibly on engineering an IRA split to be followed by a security mop-up. Adams had no convincing answer to the argument that he had relied on the British to bring him to the table, and had been let down by them.

Feeling they had been denied entry into politics, the IRA thus took the murderous step of bombing Docklands. It is a profoundly depressing thought that they did so from the same motivation which a quarter of a century ago led them to take up the gun in the first place: the conclusion that rational argument got them nowhere, that they had nothing to lose, that the only thing Britain understands is the use of force.